# Trend Forecasting With Technical Analysis

*Unleashing the Hidden Power*
*of Intermarket Analysis*
*to Beat the Market*

*Welcome aboard,*
*I hope you enjoy reading this book.*

BY LOUIS B. MENDELSOHN

*Foreword by*

JOHN J. MURPHY

TRADE • SECRETS

# Trend Forecasting With Technical Analysis

UNLEASHING THE HIDDEN POWER OF INTERMARKET
ANALYSIS TO BEAT THE MARKET

LOUIS B. MENDELSOHN
FOREWORD BY JOHN J. MURPHY

# Titles in the Trade Secrets Series

*"Intermarket analysis tools — that build and expand upon the single-market analysis methods which defined technical analysis in the late 20th century — demand serious attention."*

— Louis B. Mendelsohn

***From a Declaration of Principles jointly adopted by a Committee of the American Bar Association and a Committee of Publishers.***

This book, along with other books, are available at discounts that make it realistic to provide them as gifts to your customers, clients and staff. For more information on these long-lasting, cost-effective premiums, please call John Boyer at 800-424-4550 or e-mail him at john@traderslibrary.com.

***Printed in the United States of America.***

# Contents

**Chapter 4**

**Chapter 5**

# Foreword

They say timing is everything. Nowhere is that more true than in the financial markets. It's especially timely that Lou Mendelsohn's book on intermarket analysis should appear at the start of the new millennium. At the start of the last decade, I published a book on the same topic — *Intermarket Technical Analysis: Trading Strategies for the Global Stock, Bond, Commodity, and Currency Markets* (John Wiley & Sons, 1991). At that time, the principles of intermarket analysis seemed heretical by suggesting that single-market analysis (that had been utilized for the past century by market technicians) was no longer adequate. By the end of the decade, those seemingly radical ideas had become so accepted that the Market Technicians Association listed intermarket analysis as a branch of technical analysis.

It's hard, for example, for any market analyst who lived through the Asian crisis of 1997 to dispute the existence of global linkages — and the interdependence of all financial markets. The collapse of one Asian currency in the summer of that year caused a domino effect throughout all of Asia. Before long, Asian bankers were raising interest rates to stem the spreading currency collapse. That had a devastating effect on the Asian stock markets. That deflationary threat pushed global commodities into a free-fall and caused a massive rotation out of global stocks into U.S. Treasury bonds.

It's equally hard to argue with how the tripling of oil prices during 1999 pushed global interest rates higher and caused a bear market in bonds. That prompted the Federal Reserve Board to start raising interest rates in the middle of that year. A series of Fed tightenings over the next twelve months had a predictably restraining effect on the bull market in stocks. The impact of rising oil prices (and rising interest rates) could also be seen in sector rotations within the stock market. While rising oil prices were bullish for the energy sector during

1999, they had a predictably bearish impact on interest-rate sectors of the stock market (like financial stocks and utilities) and oil-sensitive groups like the airlines. By the middle of the year 2000, economists who had ignored the surging oil market during 1999 were crediting that surge with slowing down the U.S. economy.

In case anyone wasn't convinced a decade ago, market events since then have amply demonstrated that all markets are linked—and that a thorough market analysis has to take these intermarket relationships into consideration. Lou Mendelsohn's book takes those intermarket ideas to an even more practical level. As he correctly points out, the problem with intermarket relationships is that there are so many of them. One of his intermarket trading models incorporates as many as nine related markets. With so many markets interacting at the same time, it has become increasingly difficult for the human mind to make sense of it all. Enter neural networks.

One of Mendelsohn's greatest contributions to intermarket analysis has been his application of neural networks to the process. He shows how a neural network can take any number of related factors into consideration, analyze them, and draw some practical conclusions. And, those conclusions lead to the real benefit—winning market trades. The results of two decades of pioneering work has produced highly successful intermarket trading programs. Since I was the one who first described these intermarket principles ten years ago, I feel indebted to Mendelsohn for proving that those ideas do in fact work and that they can be profitably applied to the financial markets.

Neural networks even incorporate fundamental factors into technical and intermarket work. When talking about things like inflation and interest rates, the technical analyst sounds more like an economist than a chartist. Mendelsohn incorporates intermarket, fundamental, and technical considerations into an approach that he calls "synergistic market analysis"—a term I first heard him use when I interviewed him on CNBC™. For some purists, that may be a problem. For the rest of us, it's just another step in the evolution of technical analysis. Intermarket work has a tendency to blend the fundamental and the technical—a trend that I expect to accelerate in the new millennium. And I suspect that many of the techniques described by Mendelsohn in this pioneering work will play an important role in helping to bring about those changes.

Mendelsohn warns that what worked for technical analysts in the old century may not work in the new one. Many of us started out using pencils and rulers. We graduated to hand-held calculators before switching over to computers. Now comes neural networks. Different times demand different tools. An increasingly interdependent financial marketplace will demand an even better set of tools. It will also demand a more comprehensive approach to market analysis that incorporates all geographic regions and all markets—in other words, an intermarket approach.

—John Murphy

▲ ▲ ▲ ▲ ▲ ▲

Mr. Murphy is also the author of *Technical Analysis of the Financial Markets* and *The Visual Investor* and is the president of MurphyMorris.com.

# Preface

This book explores the application of intermarket analysis, which analyzes the relationships between financial markets and their influences on each other. It examines the critical role that intermarket analysis plays in assisting traders to identify and anticipate changes in market direction in today's globally interconnected financial markets.

These markets include stock indexes such as the Dow Jones Industrial Average℠, London's FTSE™ 100 Index, the Nasdaq Composite® Index, the Nasdaq-100 Index®, the Nikkei Stock Average® (Japan) and the Standard & Poor's 500™ Stock Index; currencies such as the British pound, Japanese yen, Swiss franc and the U.S. Dollar Index; energy markets such as crude oil, gasoline and heating oil; interest rate markets such as the eurodollar, Treasury bonds and Treasury notes; as well as individual equities.

As the burgeoning global economy of the 21st century, fostered by advancements in information technologies, contributes to the further integration of the financial markets, intermarket analysis will become an integral part of the overall field of technical analysis. Intermarket analysis empowers traders to make more effective trading decisions based upon the linkages between related financial markets. By incorporating intermarket analysis into your trading strategies, rather than limiting your scope of analysis to each individual market, these relationships and interconnections between markets will work for you rather than against you.

Suggestions are made for how intermarket analysis can be used in conjunction with traditional single-market technical indicators to provide a more comprehensive framework of analysis and broadened trading perspective. This book also introduces VantagePoint Intermarket Analysis Software which has achieved an astounding accuracy rate of nearly 80% at forecasting market direction, and offers insights into how day traders and position traders in both the futures and equity markets can use this powerful analysis tool to improve their trading performance and achieve a competitive advantage over other traders.

This book will be of interest to both experienced individual and professional traders as well as newcomers to the financial markets who want to create wealth in today's global markets.

# Introduction

After trading stocks and options for nearly a decade using various technical analysis methods, in the late 1970s, with encouragement from a physician friend who traded gold futures, I started to both day trade and position trade commodities while working professionally as a hospital administrator.

At first I subscribed to chart services, which had to be updated by hand during the week. I often joked to my wife about having to sharpen my #2 lead pencil so often, since the dullness of its point affected how my support and resistance lines were drawn, which in turn determined where I placed my stops. This was very annoying to me whenever I anticipated the market direction correctly only to miss out on a big move after being stopped out prematurely at a loss due to an ill-placed stop.

Using a hand-held calculator to compute technical indicators in the days before microcomputers, I learned the underlying theories and mathematical equations for various indicators such as moving averages, and devised mathematical shortcuts to expedite my daily calculations.

I was quite excited when I purchased my first microcomputer in the late 1970s. Before long I was teaching myself programming and writing simple software programs to automate many of these calculations.

I quickly realized that the marriage of microcomputers with technical analysis would revolutionize financial market analysis. While I had been hooked on trading and technical analysis since the early 1970s, it was the decision to apply computers to technical analysis that changed my life.

In 1979, at thirty-one years old, intent on pursuing this goal, I formed Market Technologies Corporation. A year later, with my wife Illyce's support, I left the health-care industry to devote my full attention to commodity trading, technical analysis and trading software development.

My intent was to design technical analysis software that would do more than just automate and speed up calculations I had been doing by hand each evening with a calculator. I wanted to be able to create and back-test various trading strategies to identify and forecast the market direction of the commodity markets that I traded.

In 1983, I released ProfitTaker, the first commercially available microcomputer trading software to perform strategy back-testing and optimization. With its automated back-testing capabilities, ProfitTaker represented a milestone in the evolution of computerized technical analysis.

That same year I authored a series of articles in *Futures®* magazine. In these articles I introduced the concepts of back-testing and optimization for microcomputers and discussed the impact that these innovations would have on technical analysis and trading.

Throughout the 1980s, I continued to develop more powerful trading software. I also wrote articles and collaborated on books on trading, in which I discussed the dangers of curve-fitting and over-optimization in trading strategy back-testing. Additionally, I spoke about these pitfalls in national television, radio, and magazine interviews and at financial industry conferences as an invited speaker. Before long, strategy development and back-testing had attracted the attention of traders around the world who were purchasing microcomputers for the first time.

While there was resistance from a few professionals in the financial industry whose own software had been rendered obsolete by back-testing and optimization or who felt threatened by these innovations in computerized technical analysis, I received encouragement at the time from a number of prominent technicians and traders. These included Darrell Jobman, who was editor-in-chief of *Futures* magazine, as well as Larry Williams and Jake Bernstein, who were early supporters of mine—and to whom I am grateful.

Several ProfitTaker clients subsequently became software developers themselves, and promoted competitive software programs emulating ProfitTaker's back-testing and optimization capabilities. Other existing software developers, likewise, later introduced their own versions of back-testing software, including Omega Research's Trade-Station® in 1991.

Today back-testing and optimization are so integral to single-market technical analysis that traders take these capabilities for granted. I find it somewhat amusing when I hear new traders just learning about technical analysis tell me that back-testing has always been in trading software—as if automobiles have *always* existed.

By the mid-1980s, through my technical research and observations on the markets, it had become apparent to me that single-market technical analysis methods would no longer be sufficient. Given the changes that were occurring in the financial markets due to advancements in computing and telecommunications technologies and the emerging "global economy," I realized that such methods which look internally at only one market at a time (and typically lag behind the market) were too limited.

In 1986, while searching for a way to broaden the scope of technical analysis, I developed the first commercially available intermarket analysis software for microcomputers. This program addressed market interdependencies by using a spreadsheet format to correlate movements in related markets, as well as expectations of economic statistics, with the anticipated trend direction of a target market.

The global stock market crash of October 1987 starkly affirmed my convictions about the interdependencies of the world's futures, equity and derivative markets. At that point, I was convinced that intermarket analysis would become an essential part of technical analysis as the world economies and financial markets continued to become more intertwined.

Despite my accomplishments at developing intermarket analysis software, I was not satisfied with the mathematical tools I had used to correlate market data from related markets. Then in the late 1980s after experimenting with an artificial intelligence technology known as neural networks, I concluded that they were ideally suited to the tasks of finding repetitive patterns and nonlinear relationships between a target market and related markets, and accurately forecasting market direction of the target market.

In 1991, after considerable research and development involving the application of neural networks to financial forecasting, I introduced my most advanced software program—VantagePoint Intermarket Analysis Software. VantagePoint uses neural networks to make short-term forecasts of the market direction and prices of various financial markets.

Around this same time, other technicians, including John Murphy, the technical analyst for CNBC, working independently, were also exploring intermarket relationships, primarily from an intuitive and descriptive standpoint. Their work lent further credibility among traders to the new arena of intermarket analysis.

Since the late 1980s, I have written extensively in articles and books about globalization and the integration of the world's financial markets. During this time I have continued my research and software development involving intermarket analysis, creating powerful trend forecasting trading strategies built around predicted moving averages.

The technical focus of this book's presentation is on how intermarket analysis, through the application of neural networks, can be used to forecast moving averages, making them a *leading* rather than a *lagging* technical indicator.

- **Chapter 1** discusses the globalization of the financial markets and outlines some of the major factors that are responsible for the emergence of the global economy.

- **Chapter 2** highlights the limitations of traditional technical analysis methods, particularly the emphasis on single-market analysis and the reliance upon lagging trend-following indicators.

- **Chapter 3** examines intermarket analysis as a logical extension of technical analysis and offers various ways that intermarket analysis can be used by traders to seize trading opportunities that other traders miss.

- **Chapter 4** explains the strengths and weaknesses of traditional moving averages, and shows how trend forecasting, by using neural networks applied to intermarket data, outperforms trend following.

- **Chapter 5** describes VantagePoint's market forecasting capabilities. This chapter also presents various market timing trading strategies utilizing predicted moving averages, which can be used by both day traders and position traders.

- **Chapter 6** looks at the application of neural networks to intermarket analysis and briefly outlines the basics of neural networks and how they can benefit traders in today's global markets.

- **Chapter 7** discusses the evolution of financial market analysis in the first decades of the 21st century. It suggests a comprehensive approach that I call "synergistic market analysis," which combines technical, intermarket and fundamental data into one framework for the purpose of analysis and forecasting.

In summary, this book discusses the globalization of the world's financial markets and the application of intermarket analysis in developing and implementing powerful trend forecasting and market timing trading strategies in the equity, options, derivative and futures markets.

# Trend Forecasting
# With Technical Analysis

*Unleashing the Hidden Power
of Intermarket Analysis
to Beat the Market*

# Chapter 1

# TRADING IN THE GLOBAL ECONOMY
## Have Your Trading Strategies and Profits Kept Pace?

During the last two decades of the 20th century, following the advent of microcomputers, participation in the financial markets by individual traders has grown tremendously. Trading software has proliferated as an increasing number of traders have embraced technical analysis methods for making trading decisions.

While microcomputers have become substantially faster and trading software has likewise undergone significant improvements in speed, performance and user-friendliness, the overall success rate of traders from a profitability standpoint has not materially improved. The reason, in my opinion, is that the single-market emphasis of technical analysis has not kept pace with structural changes that have occurred in the financial markets related to the emergence of the global economy.

Now, more than ever before, mass psychology and market sentiment seem to change daily, if not hourly, as market direction abruptly shifts from bullish to bearish and back again. One day a futures market or individual stock is overbought, the next day it is oversold. Today's market darling is tomorrow's ugly duckling. One day concerns over inflation are of paramount importance to traders, the next day the subject is practically forgotten as they move on to the next hot topic. Fears over interest rates and "hard landings" wax and wane as traders, with the attention span of hyperactive children, have difficulty maintaining their focus, discipline and perspective.

To the novice, these sudden shifts between greed and fear, bullishness and bearishness, optimism and pessimism, hope and resignation, seem to exist in a vacuum without rhyme or reason. Yet patterns of market behavior repeat themselves over and over again. They can be found within each market, such as the Dow Jones Industrial Average, at different periods in time, and from an intermarket perspective by analyzing relationships between related markets. Domestic and foreign markets now, more often than not, move in concert, driven by common financial, political and economic forces affecting the global economy.

Today's traders can no longer rely solely upon single-market technical analysis methods, which were designed for the more independent and less volatile domestic markets of the late 20th century.

Clearly, intermarket analysis tools which can identify reoccurring patterns within individual financial markets and between related global markets afford traders a broadened trading perspective and competitive edge in today's trading environment, which has been transformed by the mounting globalization and integration of the world's financial markets.

The rapidness of change in the global economy and the growing interdependencies between global futures and equity markets should make this topic of utmost importance to traders who want their involvement in the financial markets to be profitable, not just a costly pastime. Since the markets are a financial version of Darwin's survival of the fittest competition, intermarket analysis tools—that build and expand upon the single-market analysis methods which defined technical analysis in the late 20th century—demand serious attention.

## The Markets Are Constantly Evolving

With the emergence of a new era of global electronic communications, heralded by the first transatlantic satellite transmission in 1962, and the subsequent creation of currency, interest rate, oil and stock index futures in the 1970s and 1980s (following the decision by the United States to abandon fixed exchange rates in 1971), the world's futures and equity markets, previously distinct from one another, began to coalesce.

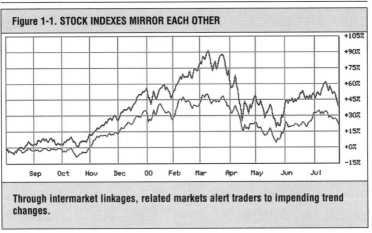

**Figure 1-1. STOCK INDEXES MIRROR EACH OTHER**

| | |
| --- | --- |
| | +105% |
| | +90% |
| | +75% |
| | +60% |
| | +45% |
| | +30% |
| | +15% |
| | +0% |
| | -15% |

Sep   Oct   Nov   Dec   00   Feb   Mar   Apr   May   Jun   Jul

Through intermarket linkages, related markets alert traders to impending trend changes.

Source: www.bigcharts.com

The proliferation of financial futures laid the early foundation for the global integration of the financial markets and for intermarket analysis to become a necessary component of technical market analysis, as volatility in interest and exchange rates, as well as in oil prices, created new opportunities and risks for speculators and hedgers, including multinational corporations.

In the past, trading was conducted on a local level within separate time zones on individual domestic stock and commodity exchanges. Now, at the dawn of the 21st century, the melding of the debt, equity, futures, derivative and options markets throughout the world continues unabated.

## The World's Futures and Equity Markets Are Linked

Take a look at the chart above (see Figure 1-1). It displays a one-year (re-scaled) comparison chart of two stock indexes. Notice how closely they track each other. Try to guess which markets they are.

If you guessed that they are the Nasdaq Composite Index and the Nasdaq-100 Index, two closely related indexes, you are half right. The one on the top of the chart is the Nasdaq Composite Index. However, the one on the bottom is not even a U.S. market. It is a Latin American Index created by Morgan Stanley Dean Witter to track growth stocks in Argentina, Brazil, Chile, Columbia, Mexico, Peru and Venezuela.

This chart illustrates the fact that even linkages between seemingly unrelated markets cannot be ignored by traders as the globalization of the financial markets continues to evolve.

Already the New York Stock Exchange®, the Nasdaq® and the Chicago Board of Trade, each mindful of the trend toward market globalization, have begun to build strategic alliances with foreign exchanges.

In the year 2000, the New York Stock Exchange announced its "Global Equity Market™" platform, which will involve alliances with various foreign exchanges, such as the Tokyo Stock Exchange, Paris-Bourse, Toronto Stock Exchange, Amsterdam Stock Exchange, Stock Exchange of Hong Kong, Australian Stock Exchange, Brazil's Bovespa, Brussels Stock Exchange and Mexico's Bolsa.

> **Linkages between seemingly unrelated markets cannot be ignored by traders as the globalization of the financial markets continues to evolve.**

At the same time the Nasdaq, through alliances with the Australian and Hong Kong exchanges, the Osaka Securities Exchange involving the creation of "Nasdaq Japan℠," the Deutsche Boerse and the London Stock Exchange in Europe, and other possible alliances in Canada and Latin America, is pursuing its own strategic plan for participation in the emerging 24-hour global financial marketplace.

Similarly, the world's two largest futures exchanges, the Chicago Board of Trade and Frankfurt's Eurex exchange, have teamed up to launch a joint electronic trading platform beginning in the year 2000. Eventually alliances such as these will allow traders to trade any financial instrument, anywhere in the world, at any time over seamless, electronic global trading platforms.

Having lived through the dismantling of the Berlin Wall, the reunification of Germany, the breakup of the U.S.S.R. and the end of the Cold War in the closing years of the last century, it would not surprise me at all if the New York Stock Exchange and the Nasdaq, for instance, were to announce the joint creation of a totally comprehensive electronic global trading network, in partnership with major stock and commodity exchanges throughout the world. Necessity is, after all, the mother of invention.

Before long, trading in the financial markets will be conducted day and night electronically, in the virtual world of cyberspace far from the brick and mortar trading floors of today's stock and futures exchanges. I can easily envision today's concepts of "after hours trading," "extended trading" and even "open outcry" becoming historical footnotes to our lexicon, just as the "buggy whip" and the "horseless carriage" were relegated at the dawn of the 20th century.

With the implementation of twenty-four-hours-a-day trading involving literally thousands of financial instruments, including esoteric ones not yet conceived, even small institutional trading organizations will need to staff their trading operations around the clock. Many individual traders, however, will suffer from market-induced insomnia, as they feel compelled to check on their market positions at all hours of the night, fearing some external cataclysmic event that triggers an abrupt change in trend direction, or worse yet an overnight worldwide meltdown of the financial markets.

High-flying Internet, technology and biotechnology stocks are already traded like commodities by electronic day traders. This stands to reason, since an uptrend is an uptrend, a trend reversal is a trend reversal and patterns repeat themselves, regardless of the label that is put on each market. It doesn't matter if it's pork bellies, orange juice, sugar, Treasury notes, the S&P 500® Index, the Swiss franc, crude oil, Intel or Amgen.

As stock index futures proliferate, index trading expands, Internet chat rooms continue to bustle with traders sharing trading tips, electronic day trading becomes recognized as a legitimate "occupation," mutual funds trade intra-day, and futures contracts on individual stocks make their debut, this worldwide intermingling of equities and futures will accelerate.

## Emerging Forces Usher in the New Global Economy

Below is a brief account of some of the more significant technological, economic, financial and political forces that are converging to bring about the globalization of the world's financial markets in the 21st century:

- Advancements in information technologies including microcomputers, satellite, software and telecommunications, which are being focused on the global expansion and commercialization of the

Internet and the development of electronic global communications and trading networks. Transactions involving the purchase and sale of financial instruments, tangible property and the raising of capital will be conducted freely, instantaneously and competitively on a worldwide level. These developments will render obsolete the concepts of local financial markets and economic nationalism.

- The expansion of global derivatives trading involving interest rate futures, stock indexes and options, and the marriage of derivatives trading with information technologies will continue to meld previously disparate markets, further increasing market interdependencies and bringing about the total internationalization of the financial markets.

- Increased global free trade and competition, and the globalization of multinational corporate financing strategies involving capital formation, hedging of foreign exchange and interest rate risk, cross-border listing of shares on multiple exchanges in different countries, corporate consolidations and cooperative competition through global alliances, and mergers and acquisitions (particularly within brokerage, investment banking and telecommunications, as well as between exchanges) across national boundaries.

- Government deregulation involving the banking, brokerage, energy, telecommunications and transportation industries. Reductions in marginal tax rates which stimulate economic activity and global competition, reallocation of capital geographically and from the public to the private sector, increased productivity, lowered costs, and spurred innovation in the development of new technologies.

- Productivity gains brought about by advancements in information technologies positively affecting the cost structure of corporate enterprises, streamlining and shortening supply chains and customer channels.

- Demographic increases in demand for financial assets and broader participation in privatized, tax-deferred profit sharing and retirement plans by baby boomers.

- The emergence of democratically elected governments, increased personal rights, free enterprise, private ownership, the privatization of formerly state-owned enterprises, the encouragement of the spirit of entrepreneurship, and the adoption of market-based economics in developing countries throughout the world, as well as the expansion of free trade with China and its likely inclusion in the World Trade Organization.

## Market Volatility and Financial Crises Are Here to Stay

All of these factors, as well as others, have ushered in a new era in which there will eventually be just one globally integrated network of financial markets into which all futures, equity and derivative markets fit as interdependent parts — like pieces in a giant jigsaw puzzle.

If you pick up a financial magazine or newspaper, or listen to financial news programs, you'll hear commentators, money managers, corporate executives, financial analysts and economists talk about a shift in the economic paradigm referred to as the "new economy" or "global economy." This is an emerging economic world order driven by global voice, data and video telecommunications, wireless m-commerce, worldwide e-commerce and an emerging electronic global financial network encompassing previously independent financial markets.

> **This is an emerging economic world order driven by global voice, data and video telecommunications, wireless m-commerce, worldwide e-commerce and an emerging electronic global financial network encompassing previously independent financial markets.**

Already, when news of an unexpected change in a government-reported economic statistic is released, terrorism occurs in the Mideast, the U.S. Federal Reserve Board or European Central Bank announces a change in interest rates, or an Asian country devalues its currency, this news is beamed around the world instantly by satellite on CNN™, CNBC and over the Internet.

Within seconds billions of dollars in financial assets can be converted and redeployed anywhere around the world electronically at the touch of a mouse button by a large institutional trader without regard to national, political, social or economic consequences, geographical considerations, or time of day. A well-placed rumor or fictitious press release, perhaps instigated by a new breed of global cyber-saboteur, can now set off an explosion of events globally with instantaneous and potentially harmful financial ramifications, even if the false information is subsequently proven to be unfounded.

The first instance of the financial market equivalent of an earthquake of global proportions occurred on October 19, 1987, as the world's futures and equity markets cascaded downward like dominoes falling against each other. Once the first domino falls, it precipitates a chain reaction that reverberates throughout the world (see Figure 1-2).

Fortunately, catastrophic damage to the world's financial markets and economies was averted in 1987, and during aftershocks from less powerful earthquakes on the financial Richter scale in the late 1990s. Yet these events set the stage for what will undoubtedly dot the world financial landscape in the 21st century, even under the most optimistic global economic scenarios.

As advancements in telecommunications and information technologies accelerate, time-sensitive global market information becomes more widely available over the Internet, and electronic day trading of stocks, futures, and even mutual funds becomes widespread, uncharted levels of intra-day and inter-day market volatility may become commonplace in the first decades of the 21st century. Suffice it to say that "normal" market sell-offs and corrections, some

---

**Figure 1-2. GLOBAL MARKETS REACT TO THE DOMINO EFFECT**

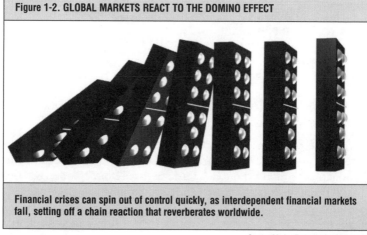

Financial crises can spin out of control quickly, as interdependent financial markets fall, setting off a chain reaction that reverberates worldwide.

Source: Market Technologies Corporation

abrupt and short lived, others protracted, but all very painful and costly to the unwary, have not been swept under the rug by the new economic paradigm.

To date, crisis control by the various sectors of the world's financial markets including stock and futures exchanges, central banks, clearing organizations, finance ministries, regulatory organizations and international banking institutions still apparently operates on an *ad hoc* basis. Presently, it is unclear whether or not the existence of a highly interdependent global communications and trading network, toward which the world's financial markets are heading, will mitigate or exacerbate global financial crises in the future.

In this climate, the difference between the financial "haves" and the "have nots" will be determined by which traders have access to the most robust intermarket analysis tools and information necessary to act decisively, particularly at the onset of instability in the financial markets.

This is especially critical for the millions of baby boomers in the United States, Europe, Japan and elsewhere, desperately in need of building and protecting their wealth to carry them through their retirement years (potentially lengthened by extended life expectancies due to breakthroughs in biotechnology).

> **Presently, it is unclear whether or not the existence of a highly interdependent global communications and trading network, toward which the world's financial markets are heading, will mitigate or exacerbate global financial crises in the future.**

With after-tax rates of return on bank deposits and money market funds barely keeping pace with inflation, and anemic returns on hard assets such as gold, the only place these baby boomers can turn to for growth potential and liquidity is the global futures and equity markets.

These realizations are what prompted me in the mid-1980s to focus my attention on the broader framework of intermarket analysis, and to develop VantagePoint as an intermarket-based market forecasting tool. VantagePoint forecasts short-term trends and prices based upon the pattern recognition capabilities of neural networks.

It answers these four important questions every trader must grapple with each day:

- Which direction is the market heading?
- How strong will the move be?
- When will the current trend lose strength, make a top or bottom and reverse direction?
- What will tomorrow's trading range be?

In Chapter 5, I will show you how VantagePoint tackles these issues. First, I want to discuss single-market technical analysis and then compare it with intermarket analysis so you can gain a better understanding of how intermarket analysis can dramatically improve your trading performance.

# Chapter 2

# SINGLE-MARKET ANALYSIS

## Trading With Tunnel Vision Can Put You on the Losing Side of a Trade

A nalysis of the behavior of financial markets for the purpose of identifying and forecasting market direction has historically and traditionally been divided into two distinct schools: fundamental analysis and technical analysis.

The rationale of fundamental analysis is to make trading decisions by forecasting market direction based upon underlying economic factors affecting a particular stock or futures market. For example, a trader sells futures contracts on U.S. Treasury notes anticipating a price decline due to expected increases in interest rates by the U.S. Federal Reserve Board; buys corn or soybean contracts based on estimates of crop damage due to expected drought conditions; or buys shares of Intel or Oracle on expectations that they will beat the Street's quarterly earnings estimates.

The premise behind technical analysis is that *all* of the internal and external factors that affect a market at any given point in time are already factored into that market's price. In other words, a market's current price is thought to reflect the rational collective judgment of all market participants, each with his own information pertaining to that market and perception of what he anticipates the market direction is likely to be in the near future.

# While Numbers Don't Lie, They Can Be Deceiving

With the assumption that the current price fully discounts all of the available information about a market and the influences or forces affecting it, technical analysis, in contrast with fundamental analysis, does not delve into any of the underlying economic factors that influence the market.

Instead, technical analysis uses various technical studies, indicators and market-forecasting theories to analyze market behavior. Historical market data such as price, volume and open interest of commodity contracts is examined to identify repetitive patterns, which, if found, can be used to determine the current market trend, anticipate future market direction, and provide price targets for entry and exit locations. This analytic process is depicted in Figure 2-1.

# The Goal Is to Forecast Market Trend Direction

While fundamental analysis and technical analysis each have their own underlying philosophical foundation and specific analytic methodologies that look at the markets from two distinct standpoints, both methods have the same goal: to identify and forecast the market trend direction of various financial markets. These include:

- Individual equities, such as Cisco Systems, Intel and Amgen.
- Stock indexes, such as the Nasdaq-100 Index, S&P 500 Index and Nikkei®.

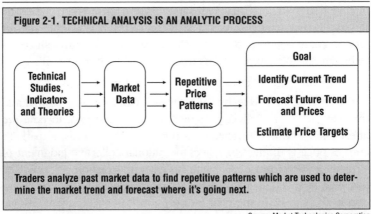

Figure 2-1. TECHNICAL ANALYSIS IS AN ANALYTIC PROCESS

Technical Studies, Indicators and Theories → Market Data → Repetitive Price Patterns →

Goal

Identify Current Trend

Forecast Future Trend and Prices

Estimate Price Targets

Traders analyze past market data to find repetitive patterns which are used to determine the market trend and forecast where it's going next.

Source: Market Technologies Corporation

- Interest rates, such as 10-year U.S. Treasury notes, 5-year U.S. Treasury notes and eurodollar.

- Currencies, such as the U.S. Dollar Index, Swiss franc and British pound.

- Energies, such as crude oil, heating oil and gasoline.

- Metals, such as gold, silver and platinum.

Through either fundamental or technical analysis, traders attempt to form expectations about the trend direction of each market, and make trading decisions with the hope of realizing a profit if their market forecasts prove to be correct.

The underlying assumption made by fundamentalists and technicians is that their methods result in superior trading performance. This has been a controversial subject over the years, with countervailing arguments that the practices of both fundamental and technical analysis are futile efforts.

From my experience over several decades as a trader and technical analyst, I am convinced that being able to make a reasonably accurate short-term trend forecast of market direction improves the outcome of the decision-making process — resulting in more profitable trading. However, even if a trader were able to make a *perfectly* accurate forecast of market direction, he would still have one final challenge to surmount. This involves *market timing*.

## You Can *Play* the Markets, or You Can *Time* the Markets

Once a trader analyzes a specific market and forms an opinion about the likely trend direction of that market, he must still decide when to get into or out of a position and at what price.

In all walks of life, timing is everything. In the financial markets, if you forecast the trend direction correctly but your timing is off (by just one day or even an hour or less) you can still end up losing money.

Historically, market timing has been particularly challenging for traders in the futures markets, due to their price volatility, low margin requirements and high degree of leverage. As the new breed of electronic day traders moves into and out of high-flying tech stocks with the same speed and indifference that futures traders buy and sell contracts on the Japanese yen or crude oil, more equity traders now concern themselves with market timing than ever before.

As a trader there is nothing more frustrating than to anticipate the trend direction correctly, get into a position slightly too soon, have the market go against you, get stopped out, and then have the market turn around and move in the direction that you expected. When this happens, you end up either sitting on the sidelines after taking a loss, or trying to chase after the market. Identifying the current trend direction, while important, is not enough. You must also be able to anticipate *when* the market is poised to make a *top* or *bottom* and change direction.

Once you can forecast the trend direction, can identify turning points, and have an expectation of the next day's price range to help you determine entry and exit locations, there's really nothing more in the way of analysis necessary. Now it's just a matter of "pulling the trigger."

## Technical Analysis Has Not Kept Pace With the Markets

If you read any recent issues of popular financial magazines you'll find numerous articles on technical analysis with current price charts and hypothetical track records, nearly identical in content to articles published in the financial press ten, twenty, and even thirty years ago!

These updated articles are undoubtedly enlightening to novice traders just beginning to learn about technical analysis and the financial markets. Remember how excited you were when you first learned how to spell "Exponential," "Fibonacci," and "Stochastic" and understood what they meant? I cannot begin to count how many dozens of articles and books on technical analysis I have read over the past several decades rehashing, for instance, the differences between various types of moving averages and comparing their effectiveness at reducing the "lag effect."

This subject was covered in detail in Perry Kaufman's *Commodity Trading Systems and Methods* originally published in 1978, and in Charles Patel's *Technical Trading Systems for Commodities and Stocks* published in

1980 — to name just two classics in my personal library. The list could go on and on.

There is a typical path that new traders seem to follow. First, they learn the ABCs of technical analysis by reading a few introductory books or magazine articles, or watching educational videos or CDs. These traders learn about price formations and chart patterns such as head-and-shoulders, flags, islands, pennants, triangles, support and resistance trend lines, gap patterns and price channels. Then the traders might attend free trading seminars in their hometowns sponsored by an e-brokerage firm or software vendor and learn about other technical indicators like candlesticks or moving averages.

Eventually new traders buy mass-marketed trading software programs that automate the calculations of various single-market indicators. After developing and testing different trading strategies built around some of these concepts, such as moving average crossover approaches, many traders begin thinking that they are on the verge of getting rich, and will soon be able to quit their day jobs and become full-time electronic day traders. This cruel fallacy has been perpetuated by alluring promotional advertisements in the financial industry for as long as I can remember.

> **Identifying the current trend direction, while important, is not enough. You must also be able to anticipate _when_ the market is poised to make a _top_ or _bottom_ and change direction.**

Many of today's traders have little, if any, personal knowledge of prior stock market routs, including the 1987 crash, not to mention the torturous decline of 1974. Just ask any veteran traders like myself about their trading experiences during the stock market debacle of 1974, when the Dow Jones Industrial Average dropped nearly 50% from its previous high, and you'll get an earful. That's when I learned the painful lesson about the psychological struggle between greed and fear, with the latter ultimately demonstrating its more powerful grip on the human psyche.

Protracted bull markets encourage novices to overestimate their skills as technicians and traders. Greed seduces traders into forming unrealistic expectations of annual market returns and the risks inherent in trading. Under such conditions traders develop a false sense of self-confidence. They begin to expect quick results, like finding the Holy Grail trading system and achieving overnight riches without having to work for it. If it were that easy, every trader would be a self-made millionaire.

Too often new traders assume that heavily promoted or inexpensive trading tools must be the ones to use, since after all so many other traders are already using them. Unfortunately, technical analysis tools are not like VCRs, where the most popular ones are usually the best.

If the masses of traders look at the markets from the same narrow single-market perspective and lose money doing so, then if you likewise limit the scope of your analysis, common sense would tell you that you should also expect to lose your money. This doesn't take a Ph.D. degree in applied mathematics to figure out. It's just high-school math: if A=B and B=C, then A=C. Yet too many newcomers to the markets start off on this losing path and stay on it until their trading capital is depleted.

> **To succeed in the financial markets, you cannot treat your trading lightly, as if it's a hobby. You must treat it like a business and that means you will need to spend time and money to succeed. Do your homework and get the best analysis tools from the get-go.**

It is foolish to think that at first you can get by using inexpensive single-market analysis tools to build up your trading account until you can afford to get the right tools. If your spouse develops a life-threatening heart condition, you wouldn't pick a cardiologist based on how cheap his fees are, with the intention that if the condition improves a little you'll switch to a more capable doctor.

Traders are bombarded with a barrage of market information from a myriad of sources including financial television channels, high-traffic financial websites and Internet chat rooms. While this explosion of information allows traders unprecedented access to the research and opinions of many reputable technical analysts, advisors and money managers, it also exposes traders to the increasingly slick and deceptive use of misinformation and "disinformation" by charlatans posing as market gurus in cyberspace.

The pervasiveness of, and ease of access to, all this information makes today's generation of traders prone to herd behavior. This herd mentality results in a psychological phenomenon referred to as "thought contagion," which contributes to industry loss statistics.

In the case of futures traders, for instance, it is reported that upwards of 95% lose their money. If the commercial airline industry had a comparable fatality record, no one in their right mind would fly, and Amtrak® would be hailed as the safest, most convenient way to travel cross-country.

To succeed in the financial markets, you cannot treat your trading lightly, as if it's a hobby. You must treat it like a business and that means you will need to spend time and money to succeed. Do your homework and get the best analysis tools from the get-go, or don't bother trading and take a trip to Las Vegas instead. You'll have a lot more fun and a lot less aggravation.

## Traders Need to Take Off Their Blinders

While even novice traders readily admit that the world's financial markets are interconnected, and acknowledge intermarket dynamics as important factors in determining the trend direction of individual markets, an overwhelming percentage of traders, particularly those new to the futures and equity markets in the last few years and especially those with limited capital, are still either unfamiliar with intermarket analysis or just don't know how to incorporate it into their trading.

These traders hear and read every day about how the markets are interconnected and affect each other—but don't really know how to make the connection themselves. So, like ostriches with their heads in the sand, they stick with single-market analysis methods and lagging indicators, until it's too late.

They continue to wear restrictive technical analysis blinders, content to focus their attention on only one market at a time, as though each market trades in total isolation. This results in an incomplete perception of what is really happening—and more importantly what is *about to happen*—in the markets that they are trading.

No wonder so many traders run for cover like scared rabbits when the markets get choppy or there is a sudden trend reversal. If this is how you are currently performing your analysis, you are making your trading decisions in an intermarket "vacuum." This can only lead to failure. If you have a relatively small account to work with, your situation is even more precarious because you have little margin of error before your capital is exhausted.

## The Blind Men and the Elephant

The "Six Blind Men and the Elephant" parable reminds me of the limitations of single-market analysis. Each of the men touched one part of an object that they had discovered in hopes of determining what it was. Here's how they each described what they had found:

| | |
|---|---|
| | The first blind man insisted it was some type of spear. It was sharp, hard, coarse, and sturdy. |
| | The second blind man concluded it was some type of rope or whip. |
| | The third blind man thought it was some type of a wall, since it had a rough texture and was very firm. |
| | The fourth blind man decided that they had found some type of an animal, probably a large snake, since it was long, easy to bend and had a strange texture. |
| | The fifth blind man thought that they had found some type of plant. It felt like a large leaf because of its texture and size. |
| | The sixth blind man was convinced that they had found a log or branch of a tree, since he had already heard from one of the other men that the object felt like a leaf. |

They were all wrong. They had each only touched a small part of an elephant and formed incorrect conclusions based on their limited observations. The financial markets are no different. If this had been a trade, it would have been a losing one! While an analysis of each individual market is still important, it is no longer sufficient because it fails to take into consideration the whole picture.

As the global integration of the financial markets continues to extend throughout the financial industry, traders who limit their analysis to a single market's past prices (or rely exclusively upon subjective chart pattern analysis or linear forecasting methods such as trend lines) for clues regarding a market's future trend direction, will be at a severe competitive disadvantage. These traders will undoubtedly end up watching their trading accounts dwindle, while informed traders who incorporate intermarket analysis into their trading strategies will be in a position to amass substantial wealth.

In the next chapter, I will discuss intermarket analysis in more detail, and show how your trading can profit from it.

# Chapter 3

## INTERMARKET ANALYSIS
### Seizing Trading Opportunities
### in a Shrinking World

Over the past few decades, when the financial markets were less volatile and tended to trade independently of one another, single-market methods of analysis were the mainstay of technical analysis and rightfully so. However, at this juncture, a narrow characterization of the markets, with its focus (if not preoccupation) on the inward analysis of each individual market, is much too limited. Traders need to expand their perspective to take into consideration external factors that affect each market.

Here's a simple analogy. Imagine yourself as a licensed pilot preparing to fly your private plane from New York City to Washington, D.C., just before dusk one summer evening. Everything on your preflight checklist indicates that all of the plane's *internal* operating systems are functioning properly, including visual fuel and oil checks, control movements, altimeter, compasses, flaps, mags and engine runup. However, you neglect to inquire about one critical *external* factor: the flight service in-route weather briefing.

In effect, by ignoring the external environmental context in which your plane will be flying, you are implicitly assuming that either the weather conditions will be favorable, or will not adversely affect your flight. This could make for a "hard landing" (no pun intended) if in fact the weather conditions prove unfavorable for such a flight.

Is trading Treasury notes, crude oil, the Nasdaq-100 Index or the Japanese yen any different if you are ignoring the broader intermarket forces affecting these individual markets?

The cliché "what you don't know can't hurt you" is false. Ignorance is not bliss when it comes to piloting planes or trading futures or equities. If you have the right tools, which give you pertinent information, you will be able to make calculated decisions; if you don't, you are just gambling, either with your life or with your hard-earned money.

Sure, it is worthwhile to analyze the behavior of each individual market. I still do a lot of that in my trading. Failed double tops, broken trend lines and prices cutting above or below their 50-day or 200-day moving average are still useful indicators of market direction, if for no other reason than the fact that they are followed by so many traders and acted upon through mass psychology. However, it is not good enough to look only at each individual market by itself.

Popular single-market technical analysis indicators such as moving averages and chart pattern formations are *lagging indicators* which look *retrospectively* at an individual market's past data in an effort to identify reoccurring patterns which can then be extrapolated into the future. This type of analysis really boils down to looking at where the market has been, and trying to *guess* where it is going.

Since the objective of technical analysis is trend identification and forecasting, it would stand to reason that this goal could best be achieved by working with *leading indicators* that *anticipate* changes in trend direction.

I prefer to forecast market direction *prospectively* in a manner that captures the character and nature of today's interdependent financial markets. This can be accomplished by using intermarket analysis tools comprised of leading indicators that forewarn whether an existing trend is likely to continue or is about to change direction. This takes the guesswork out of trading.

## Intermarket Analysis in the Equity and Commodity Markets

Intermarket analysis had its genesis in both the equity and commodity markets. Traditional technical analysis within the equity markets has historically looked at relationships among individual stocks, sectors and broad market indexes.

Additionally, comparisons between the debt and equity markets have been made, as the effects of fluctuating interest rates, inflationary expectations, and central bank policies have played an increasingly important role in determining the market direction of equities. More recently, comparisons between broad market indexes representing various stock markets around the world have been made.

Intermarket analysis within the equity markets include the following comparisons:

- Domestic broad market indexes to one another.
- Market sectors to the broad market indexes.
- Individual stocks to broad market indexes.
- Individual stocks to one another within a sector.
- The relationship of price, time and volume to one another.
- The advance/decline line compared to the performance of broad market indexes.
- Movements in interest rates to movements in stock indexes such as the relationship between 10-year Treasury notes and the S&P 500 Index, as shown in Figure 3-1.

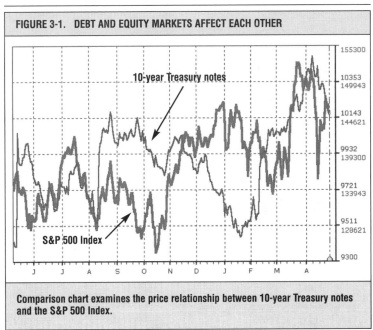

**FIGURE 3-1.  DEBT AND EQUITY MARKETS AFFECT EACH OTHER**

Comparison chart examines the price relationship between 10-year Treasury notes and the S&P 500 Index.

Source: VantagePoint Intermarket Analysis Software

- Stock indexes, such as the Nikkei 225 and FTSE 100, are compared to similar market indexes in other countries such as U.S. stock indexes including The Dow℠ or Nasdaq.

Figure 3-2 depicts a comparison chart of the Nikkei and the Dow Jones Industrial Average, showing how these two global markets behave relative to one another.

By their nature, the commodity markets have historically lent themselves to intermarket analysis. With both a cash market and numerous futures contract months existing simultaneously on a given commodity, and with such closely related commodity complexes as the grains, meats, currencies, interest rates, stock indexes, metals and energies, intra-commodity and inter-commodity spread analysis has been an integral part of technical analysis of the commodity markets for decades.

Spreads between futures markets of related instruments are looked at to gain additional insight into market direction. These include:

- The "NOB" (Notes Over Bonds) spread between 10-year Treasury notes and 30-year Treasury bonds.

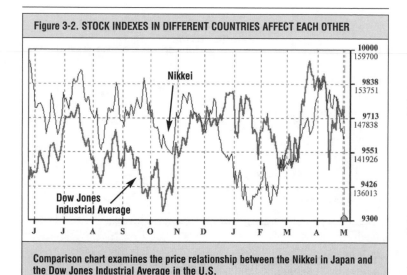

Figure 3-2. STOCK INDEXES IN DIFFERENT COUNTRIES AFFECT EACH OTHER

Comparison chart examines the price relationship between the Nikkei in Japan and the Dow Jones Industrial Average in the U.S.

Source: VantagePoint Intermarket Analysis Software

- The "TED" (Tbills-Eurodollar) spread between 90-day Treasury bills and the 90-day eurodollar.

- Spreads between bonds and the Bridge/CRB® Futures Price Index, the U.S. Dollar Index, gold and crude oil, to name a few.

Intermarket comparisons between futures and the equity markets highlight short-term confirmation or divergence, which provides insight into impending changes in market trend direction. Futures can be monitored as an early barometer of the equity markets. Futures on the S&P 500 Index, Treasury bonds and notes, as well as other financial futures markets including crude oil, the Bridge/CRB Futures Price Index and the U.S. Dollar Index are increasingly looked upon as having strong influences on the equity markets.

For instance, higher Bridge/CRB Futures Price Index prices, suggesting higher inflation down the road for various commodities, tend to drive Treasury notes prices lower (and interest rates higher) which is also negative for those sectors of the equity markets linked to these commodities including the agricultural, banking, energy, metals and industrials sectors.

Globally related markets can be analyzed with regard to their confirmation or divergence from one another over time, in response to various global and domestic economic considerations. For instance, changes in interest rates (effected by the U.S. Federal Reserve Board, European Central Bank or the Bank of Japan), currency devaluations or sudden spikes in crude oil prices have a pronounced effect on futures and equity markets worldwide.

Intermarket analysis between like debt instruments in different countries also offers worthwhile cues concerning future global trends in interest rates. For example, spreads involving government notes and bonds from various countries can be examined with respect to each other, as global arbitrage of interest rates tends to keep international debt markets synchronized.

## No Market Is Exempt From Globalization

Every market, both domestically and internationally, now appears to have some effect on every other market, however seemingly distant and unrelated. A thorough analysis of the outlook of any one market is now incomplete without looking at it within an intermarket context.

Figure 3-3 shows nine related markets that are examined by VantagePoint's 10-year Treasury notes program. As the software continues to be refined as part of my firm's ongoing research effort to increase VantagePoint's predictive accuracy, related markets will change and more will be added.

## Why Markets Converge or Diverge

Although there are direct and inverse relationships that on the surface appear to link markets to one another when they are examined two at a time, these linkages are neither fixed nor linear in nature. Instead they are dynamic, and have varying strengths, as well as varying leads and lags to one another that shift over time.

With the increased emphasis today on on-line day trading (where twenty minutes is considered long term) novice traders expect the effects on a market from related markets to be instantaneous. Traders think that all they have to do is look at what Treasury bonds or notes are doing at any moment in time to get cues on what the stock market will do next. However, this is not how the financial markets work. Sometimes the order of cause and effect is reversed, with stocks seeming to lead bonds and notes while at other times the Treasurys appear to lead stocks. Like the chicken and egg dilemma, it is very hard to discern which comes first.

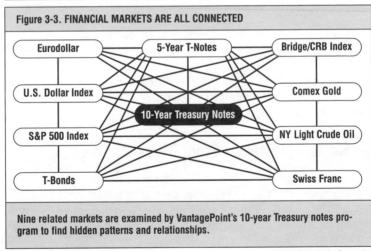

**Figure 3-3. FINANCIAL MARKETS ARE ALL CONNECTED**

| Eurodollar | 5-Year T-Notes | Bridge/CRB Index |
| U.S. Dollar Index | | Comex Gold |
| | 10-Year Treasury Notes | |
| S&P 500 Index | | NY Light Crude Oil |
| T-Bonds | | Swiss Franc |

Nine related markets are examined by VantagePoint's 10-year Treasury notes program to find hidden patterns and relationships.

Source: Market Technologies Corporation

# Intermarket Dynamics Must Be Taken Into Consideration

Traders are still too preoccupied with the inward analysis of each market, ignoring the interdependencies of the financial markets and their effects on one another, which have become more pronounced as the markets have become increasingly globalized.

Additionally, scant progress has been made at objectively (quantitatively) rather than subjectively (qualitatively) identifying repetitive patterns in market data, necessary to perform effective forecasting.

Now it is imperative for traders to adopt an intermarket perspective and incorporate intermarket analysis into their trading strategies, in order to deal with the global financial markets *as they really exist*.

If you look at the planet Saturn through an inexpensive, low-powered telescope, you won't see the rings that surround it. They are there, but the tool you are using doesn't have the capability to discern them. The same is true for how you look at the markets. While the interconnections are there, you may not see them — *but other traders do*.

Failing to factor into their trading strategies the linkages between related markets, many traders remain oblivious to the underlying intermarket forces or *market synergy* that increasingly affects price movements in today's global markets. Unquestionably, this narrow analytic perspective contributes to the financial fatality rate, among both experienced and novice traders.

I think it is absurd when I hear traders say that having an accurate short-term forecast of market direction would be of no benefit to them in their trading. These traders obviously do not understand the basic purpose of technical analysis. They have become so caught up with back-testing number crunching on each individual market that they have lost sight of the forest for the trees.

## Early Attempts at Intermarket Analysis Fall Short

Due to the complexity of the dynamic interactions between financial markets, it is difficult for the average trader to perform even rudimentary intermarket analysis. Nevertheless, technical analysts have devised various ways to do so. Here are some popular, yet in my opinion somewhat ineffective, ways that analysts and traders attempt to quantify the effects of related markets:

- Price charts on two markets are compared to one another, and the difference between the two markets' prices on a minute-by-minute, hourly, daily, weekly, or monthly basis is calculated and presented graphically or numerically, as an indication of future market direction.

- A ratio of the prices representing two markets is calculated and presented graphically or numerically to show how the two markets have behaved relative to one another in the past, to help anticipate what they are likely to do in the future.

- A statistical linear correlation analysis on two markets is performed. This approach measures the degree to which the prices of one market move in relation to the prices of the second market. The mathematical indicator used to measure correlation is known as a statistical correlation coefficient.

## Tracking Related Markets Pays Off

As the number of markets to be explored from an intermarket perspective increases, the effectiveness of using any of the previously mentioned methods rapidly diminishes. These methods of analyzing intermarket relationships are limited to price comparisons of only two markets at a time, often assuming incorrectly that the effects of one market on another occur without any leads or lags. In addition, such methods presuppose the effects are linear in nature in a sort of one-to-one causal relationship. This, too, is not realistic with respect to how the global financial markets function.

Leads and lags exist between domestic and international economic activity and the financial markets, and between related domestic and global financial markets. Sometimes the effects may not be discernible for days, weeks or months, as in the case of inflationary pressures or the implementation of central bank monetary policies that take time to work their way through the global economy.

To examine the multiple effects of as few as five or ten related markets simultaneously on a target market, methods such as linear correlation analysis and subjective chart pattern analysis quickly reveal their inadequacy as forecasting tools.

For most traders it is just too difficult and time consuming to keep up with more than two or three related markets simultaneously and to figure out how they influence each other. Two or three charts can be "eyeballed" at the same time, or a linear correlation can be calculated between two markets at a time. However, these approaches *fail to capture* the **simultaneous combined effects** of numerous related markets on a specific target market.

## Full Field of Vision Is Critical

You can get a sense of the difference between single-market analysis and intermarket analysis if you put a hand over one of your eyes and try walking around the room. With only one eye open, your field of vision is limited and your ability to visualize your surroundings is severely restricted. This is how most traders make their trading decisions, with a narrow focus on each market in isolation. Next drop your hand and walk around the room with both eyes open. Now you are really benefiting from your full field of vision. Don't you think you would have an advantage if you tackle your trading the same way—with both eyes wide open?

Here's a different way to visualize the added depth that intermarket analysis brings to bear on your trading decisions. Consider the case of the Captain of the ocean liner *Savvy Trader*, navigating the treacherous waters of the north Atlantic early last century. Trying to pick the safest route to his destination, he scanned the horizon for hazards; he took notice of wind speed, air temperature, wave frequency and height.

At a distance, he spotted a large floating chunk of ice. Carefully plotting its speed and direction over time, he extrapolated its movement and concluded that the ice wasn't a threat to his ship. That night, however, the Captain was awakened by a loud crash. The iceberg had slammed into his ship. The Captain was confused, shocked and angry.

He had not anticipated that this would happen. While meticulously examining the conditions *on the surface*, he was unaware of critical conditions *beneath the surface*. The bulk of the massive iceberg had been hidden from view; warming water temperatures had melted the ice, increasing its speed. Changes in underwater currents had affected its direction much more than surface winds. At the time (before sonar, infrared and satellite imaging were available), the Captain did not have tools capable of predicting the direction of the iceberg.

A similar situation confronts today's traders who limit themselves to single-market analysis and lagging indicators to determine market direction. What they are doing is not wrong; it's simply insufficient. Intermarket analysis tools give today's traders the same edge in their decisions that sonar gives today's ship captains.

You do not need to throw the baby out with the bath water, though. I am not suggesting that you should stop performing single-market technical analysis or abandon the use of trend following methods that have played a central role in technical analysis for decades.

Many popular single-market technical indicators are useful to one degree or another to analyze internal market behavior. However, they are most effective when used in combination with intermarket analysis to get a three-dimensional view of each market. This is not a case of "either-or." Intermarket analysis should, at the very least, be used as a confirmation filter to single-market indicators. In this manner, marginal trades can be filtered out and avoided.

This distinction can be visualized by contrasting the rectangle on the left side of Figure 3-4, representing single-market analysis, with the three-dimensional cube on the right side representing intermarket analysis.

---

**Figure 3-4. INTERMARKET ANALYSIS GIVES MORE DEPTH TO YOUR ANALYSIS**

**Single-market analysis looks only at each market by itself. Intermarket analysis adds a third dimension by taking into consideration the effects of related markets.**

Source: Market Technologies Corporation

Intermarket analysis builds upon the strengths of single-market analysis, adding another dimension to the analytic framework so that the behavior of each market can be analyzed internally as well as within a broader intermarket context.

In Figure 3-5, I have outlined some of the distinctions, from a practical trading standpoint, between intermarket analysis and single-market analysis.

| Figure 3-5 INTERMARKET ANALYSIS BROADENS THE SCOPE OF SINGLE-MARKET ANALYSIS AND OVERCOMES MANY OF ITS LIMITATIONS | |
| --- | --- |
| **Intermarket Analysis With Trend Forecasting Indicators** | **Single-Market Analysis With Trend Following Indicators** |
| ➤ Looks at multiple markets simultaneously. Analyzes their effects on a target market. | ➤ Looks at one market at a time. |
| ➤ Leads the market, pinpointing trading opportunities as they are about to unfold. | ➤ Lags the market, causing traders to miss the start of new trends. |
| ➤ Traders can enter and exit trades just as the trend is changing. | ➤ Trades are often triggered several days after the trend has changed direction. |
| ➤ Trends are identified as they are developing so traders catch a bigger portion of each move. | ➤ Often gives back a large portion of profits, sometimes turning a profitable trade into a losing trade. |
| ➤ Stops are placed based on how related markets are affecting the market being traded. | ➤ Stop placements are determined by looking at the market being traded, often based on commonly used indicators such as trend lines, which tend to cluster stops near one another. |
| ➤ False trading signals are minimized because the full picture is taken into consideration, not just a small piece of it. | ➤ False signals are common during sideways markets resulting in frequent losing trades. |
| Differences between intermarket analysis and single-market analysis highlight the importance of adding intermarket analysis to your trading arsenal. | |

Source: Market Technologies Corporation

# Intermarket Analysis: In the Right Place at the Right Time

A formal, quantitative methodology to implement intermarket analysis, such as I have applied since 1991 within VantagePoint, is neither a radical departure from traditional technical analysis, nor an attempt to undermine or replace it. Intermarket analysis, in my opinion, is simply the next logical developmental stage in the evolution of technical analysis, given the global nature of today's interdependent, highly complex economies and integrated financial markets.

> **I found the best way to implement intermarket analysis is through the use of neural networks. They excel at finding reoccurring patterns and relationships between related markets, as well as patterns within a single market. Once found, these patterns are used to make highly accurate forecasts of market direction.**

If you need to dig a hole in the ground that is a foot deep and a foot square, you wouldn't do it with a teaspoon. Similarly, if you want to stir a cup of coffee, you wouldn't use a spade. You've got to use the right tool for the job. Today's markets are interdependent and interconnected. That means you need to perform intermarket analysis. Let's call a spade a spade —single-market analysis by itself is simply not adequate, period.

I found the best way to implement intermarket analysis is through the use of neural networks. They excel at finding reoccurring patterns and relationships between related markets, as well as patterns within a single market. Once found, these patterns are used to make highly accurate forecasts of market direction.

By analyzing the effects of related markets (particularly the futures markets which are inherently oriented toward anticipating future price levels), important early warnings of impending changes in market direction can be gleaned from intermarket data well before these changes begin to show up on the charts of traders who limit the scope of their analysis to each individual market.

VantagePoint, for example, using extensive intermarket data, forecasts the market direction for the next two and four days and forewarns, through its "Neural Index" indicator, whether a target market is expected to make a *top* or *bottom* within the next two days. This is all done automatically through the pattern recognition and forecasting capabilities of neural networks, which I will discuss in Chapter 6.

Let's face it, even my eleven-year-old son can look at a bar chart and tell you what happened in the stock market yesterday and over the last few days or weeks. Hindsight is 20/20; but you can only profit by having foresight. You cannot make money tomorrow or next week based on what happened yesterday or last week. You can only make money if on a consistent basis you can anticipate, with reasonable accuracy, what is going to happen in the near future.

If you had Tuesday's *Investor's Business Daily®* or *The Wall Street Journal®* available to you every Monday morning with your coffee — one day in advance — you could quickly become the wealthiest person in the world. Why? Because you would have 100% accurate information on the following day's prices and would know exactly what to expect next.

## The Only Thing Certain Is Uncertainty Itself

Unfortunately, it is no more possible to make 100% accurate forecasts of the financial markets than to get *The Wall Street Journal* one day in advance. Forecasting inherently involves mathematical probabilities, not certainty. However, a market forecast does not need to be perfect to tilt the odds in your favor.

To have a substantial competitive advantage over other traders, all you need is a reliable forecast that can consistently beat a coin toss. VantagePoint's nearly 80% predictive accuracy at forecasting short-term market direction gives you more than enough edge over other traders.

Widely used technical indicators can be applied to intermarket analysis in innovative ways. I have been very successful in accomplishing this with VantagePoint, in which neural networks make short-term forecasts of moving averages.

In the next chapter I will discuss moving averages, showing you how I turned them into a powerful leading indicator within Vantage-Point through the use of intermarket analysis and neural networks.

# Chapter 4

## TODAY'S MARKETS HAVE CHANGED

### Why Trend Forecasting Beats Trend Following and How Traders Can Profit

Moving averages are one of the most popular technical indicators used to identify the trend direction of financial markets. Moving averages form the basis of a myriad of single-market trend following trading strategies, ranging from the popular 4-9-18-day moving average "crossover" approach to the widely followed 50-day and 200-day simple moving averages used to assess the market trend direction of broad market indexes and individual stocks.

Figure 4-1, on the next page, depicts the Dow Jones Industrial Average with its 200-day moving average superimposed on the daily price chart. This indicator is used extensively by technicians and traders as an indication of The Dow's trend direction. When The Dow closes above its 200-day moving average, the market is considered to be in an uptrend. When The Dow closes below its 200-day moving average, the uptrend is considered to be "broken" as a bearish sentiment permeates the market.

Moving averages are precisely calculated according to specific mathematical formulae. This makes moving averages an objective way to determine the current trend direction of a market, and anticipate its most likely future direction. This is in sharp contrast to subjective approaches to trend identification based on visual chart analysis of reoccurring patterns such as head-and-shoulder formations, flags, triangles and pennants, etc.

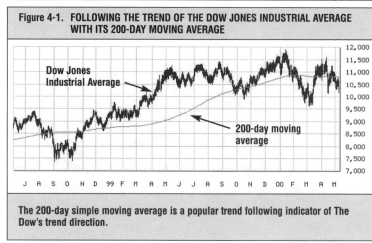

**Figure 4-1. FOLLOWING THE TREND OF THE DOW JONES INDUSTRIAL AVERAGE WITH ITS 200-DAY MOVING AVERAGE**

The 200-day simple moving average is a popular trend following indicator of The Dow's trend direction.

Source: www.bigcharts.com

Mathematically, moving averages filter out the random "noise" in market data by smoothing out fluctuations and short-term volatility in price movement. Graphically superimposing a moving average on a price chart makes it easy to visualize the underlying trend within the data.

## Moving Averages Are Lagging Indicators

However, traditional moving averages have one very serious deficiency. They are a "lagging" technical indicator. This means that moving averages, due to their mathematical construction (averaging prices over a number of prior periods), tend to trail behind the current market price. In fast moving markets, where the price is on the verge of rising or falling precipitously, this lag effect can become very pronounced and costly.

The shorter the length of a moving average, the more sensitive it will be to short-term price fluctuations. The longer the length of a moving average, the less sensitive it will be to abrupt price fluctuations. Therefore, short moving averages lag the market less than long moving averages, but are less effective than long moving averages at smoothing or filtering out the noise.

Trades based upon moving averages are often late to get into and out of the market compared to the point at which the market's price actually makes a *top* or *bottom* and begins to move in the opposite direction.

Figure 4-2 depicts a chart of daily prices of the U.S. Dollar Index compared to its 10-day simple moving average. Because of the steep price increase prior to the market making a top, the moving average actually continues to increase in value, even as the market begins to drop before cutting the moving average from above to below.

Depending on the price movement and the type and size of moving average used, this "response" delay can be financially devastating under extreme circumstances, such as waking up one morning and finding yourself on the wrong side of an abrupt trend reversal involving a lock-limit futures position.

The lag effect, which to date has been the Achilles' heel of moving averages, has presented a challenge to technical analysts and traders for decades. Extensive research has been directed at finding ways to reduce the lag, while at the same time retaining the benefits of moving averages.

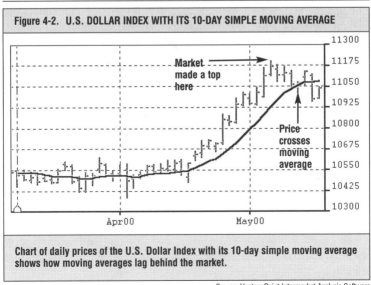

**Figure 4-2. U.S. DOLLAR INDEX WITH ITS 10-DAY SIMPLE MOVING AVERAGE**

Chart of daily prices of the U.S. Dollar Index with its 10-day simple moving average shows how moving averages lag behind the market.

Source: VantagePoint Intermarket Analysis Software

To accomplish these two goals, numerous variations of moving averages have been devised. Each has its own mathematical construction, effectiveness at identifying the underlying trend of a market and ability to overcome the lag effect. The three most common types of moving averages relied upon by technical analysts and traders for decades are the simple, weighted and exponential moving averages.

### Simple Moving Averages

A simple moving average is the arithmetic "mean" or average of a price series over a selected time period. As the market moves forward in time, the oldest price is removed from the moving average calculation and replaced by the most recent price. This allows the moving average to "move," thereby keeping pace with changes in the market's price. A simple moving average lags behind the market because it gives equal weight to each period's price. This limitation is what has prompted the use of weighted and exponential moving averages.

### Weighted and Exponential Moving Averages

A weighted moving average attempts to reduce the lag by giving more weight to recent prices, thereby allowing the moving average to respond more quickly to current market conditions. The most popular version is the linearly weighted moving average.

An exponential moving average, like a weighted moving average, gives more weight to recent prices, while differing from a weighted average in other respects.

## Moving Averages Are Popular — But Something's Missing

Virtually every book on technical analysis devotes at least one chapter to moving averages, describing detailed accounts of the various means that technicians have devised to reduce the lag effect.

While each type of moving average has its own strengths and weaknesses at smoothing the data and reducing the lag, none of them, by virtue of being based solely on past single-market price data, have been successful at eliminating the lag.

Using microcomputers and strategy back-testing software, since the early 1980s traders have optimized the sizes of moving averages in an effort to best fit them to each specific target market. For instance, the moving average length selected for Intel might be entirely different than for Applied Materials, Treasury notes or the Japanese yen.

In fact, the moving average length selected for a specific market at one point in time or under certain market conditions is often different than at other times or under other conditions. These observations encourage traders to re-optimize moving averages periodically (and sometimes too frequently), in a futile attempt to keep them responsive to current market conditions.

## Moving Average Crossovers Lead to Whipsaws

Moving averages can be used as building blocks in more complex technical indicators, in which, for instance, two moving averages are compared to one another. This is done either by subtracting the value of one moving average from the other or by dividing one moving average value by the other. Traditional moving average "crossover" strategies are extensively relied upon by traders to discern market direction.

> **Traditional moving average crossover strategies are quite effective at filtering out market noise and identifying the current market direction in trending markets.**

A typical moving average crossover approach, for instance, involves the calculation of two simple moving averages of different lengths, such as a 5-day and a 10-day moving average. When the short moving average value is greater than the long moving average value, the trend is assumed to be *up*. When the short moving average value is less than the long moving average value, the trend is assumed to be *down*.

Traditional moving average crossover strategies are quite effective at filtering out market noise and identifying the current market direction in trending markets. However, in highly volatile, or choppy, nontrending sideways markets, or even in trending markets when using very short moving averages (which may be overly sensitive to short term price fluctuations), these approaches tend to generate faulty trading signals. This results in repeated "whipsaws" which can rack up trading losses as alternating buy and sell signals are triggered each time the moving averages crisscross one another.

Some trading strategies attempt to reduce the lag by comparing an actual price, such as the daily close, with a moving average value for trend determination. Other strategies attempt to minimize whipsaws by using bands surrounding the moving averages, or by including additional moving averages to filter out false trading signals, both of which I implemented in ProfitTaker in the early 1980s. The number of permutations and combinations of what can be done with moving averages is staggering.

Figure 4-3 shows the U.S. Dollar Index with its 5-day and 10-day simple moving averages superimposed on the daily price chart. In this case, trading decisions might be based on the short moving average crossing the long moving average (or on the close crossing one or both of the moving averages). Notice how the turning points in the moving averages lag behind the turning points in the market itself.

A basic assumption underlying the application of moving averages is that a trend once in motion tends to persist. Therefore, until the

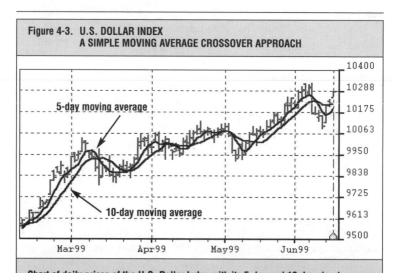

**Figure 4-3. U.S. DOLLAR INDEX**
**A SIMPLE MOVING AVERAGE CROSSOVER APPROACH**

Chart of daily prices of the U.S. Dollar Index with its 5-day and 10-day simple moving averages shows how short averages are more responsive than long averages, but both lag behind the market.

Source: VantagePoint Intermarket Analysis Software

long moving average is penetrated by the short moving average, for instance, in the direction opposite from the prevailing trend, the prevailing trend is assumed to still be intact.

## Computing a Simple Moving Average Is Easy

The 5-day simple moving average of closes as of today's close is calculated by adding up the values of the most recent five days' closing prices and dividing by 5.

Mathematically this involves adding up or "summing" the closing prices for $\text{Day}_t$ + $\text{Day}_{t-1}$ + $\text{Day}_{t-2}$ + $\text{Day}_{t-3}$ + $\text{Day}_{t-4}$, in which $\text{Day}_t$ is today's Close, $\text{Day}_{t-1}$ is yesterday's Close . . . and $\text{Day}_{t-4}$ is the Close of the trading day four days ago. Then the sum is divided by 5.

Figure 4-4 shows a series of five daily closing prices of the Nasdaq Composite Index and the computation of its 5-day simple moving average.

This same approach can be used to calculate simple moving averages of various lengths, such as a 10-day moving average, a 50-day moving average or a 200-day moving average. Additionally, prices other than the close can be used in the computation. For instance, a simple moving average can be computed on the High + Low divided by 2, or on the Open + High + Low + Close divided by 4. Even intraday moving averages can be computed for various time intervals.

---

**Figure 4-4. THE NASDAQ COMPOSITE INDEX**
**CALCULATING A 5-DAY SIMPLE MOVING AVERAGE OF CLOSES**

| | Closing Prices | |
|---|---|---|
| $\text{Day}_{t-4}$ | 3384.73 | |
| $\text{Day}_{t-3}$ | 3499.58 | **17,738.59 ÷ 5 = 3547.72** |
| $\text{Day}_{t-2}$ | 3529.06 | **= Today's 5-Day Moving** |
| $\text{Day}_{t-1}$ | 3607.65 | **Average of Closes** |
| $\text{Day}_t$ | 3717.57 | |
| | **17,738.59** | |

Computing a simple moving average is easy. Just add up the prices and divide by the number of days.

Source: Market Technologies Corporation

# Displaced Moving Averages: Close But "No Cigar"

One intriguing type of moving average that attempts to overcome the lag effect is the displaced moving average. Ordinarily when computing a moving average and using it as part of a trading strategy, the moving average value for Day $_t$ is plotted on a price chart in alignment with the closing price of Day $_t$.

When this is done the lag is evident visually on the price chart as the market trends higher, for instance, and the moving average trails below the most recent prices. Similarly, if the market reverses abruptly and starts to trend lower, the moving average lags above the most recent prices and briefly may even continue to increase in value as the market declines.

A displaced moving average attempts to minimize the lag by "displacing" or "shifting" the moving average value forward in time on the chart. So, in other words, a 5-day moving average value calculated on Day $_t$ (today), instead of being plotted in alignment with the price of Day $_t$, might be shifted forward (to the right) so it is plotted on the price chart to correspond with Day $_{t+2}$ (the day after tomorrow). Similarly, a 10-day moving average might be shifted forward four days into the future from today to correspond with Day $_{t+4}$.

The implicit assumption behind displacing a moving average is that the future period's actual moving average value (which is yet to be determined) will turn out to be equal to today's actual moving average value. This is, of course, a very simplistic and unrealistic assumption regarding the *estimate* of the future period's moving average value. However, it is, nevertheless, a forecast—not just a linear extrapolation from past price data such as one achieves by extending a support or resistance line to the right of a price chart.

## A New Way to Forecast Moving Averages

The fact that despite their limitations moving averages continue to be widely used by traders is testimony that moving averages are recognized in the financial industry as an important quantitative trend identification tool. Yet, at the same time, the inherent lagging nature of moving averages continues to be a very serious shortcoming that has dogged technical analysts and traders for decades.

If this deficiency were somehow overcome, moving averages could rank as the most effective trend identification and forecasting technical indicator in financial market analysis.

Since traditional moving averages are computed using only past price data—the price for today, for yesterday, and so on—turning points in the moving averages will always lag behind turning points in the market.

For instance, to compute a 5-day simple moving average as of today's close, today's close plus the previous four days' closes are used in the computation, as depicted previously in Figure 4-4 (see page 65). These prices are already known since they have all already occurred. The problem with this computation, from a practical trading standpoint, is that the moving average lags behind what is *about to happen* in the market tomorrow.

For a trader trying to anticipate what the market direction will be tomorrow, and determine entry and exit points for tomorrow's trading, any lag, however small, may be financially ruinous given today's market volatility.

By comparison, a predicted 5-day simple moving average for two days in the future, based upon the most recent three days' closing prices up through and including today's close (which are known values), plus the next two days' closing prices (which have not yet occurred) would have, by definition, no lag, if the *exact* closing prices for the next two trading days were known in advance.

**No one will ever be able to predict the financial markets perfectly—not now, not in a hundred years. Through financial forecasting, though, mathematical expectations of the future can be formulated.**

Unfortunately, there is no such thing as 100% accuracy when it comes to forecasting market direction or prices for even one or two days in advance. No one will ever be able to predict the financial markets perfectly—not now, not in a hundred years. Through financial forecasting, though, mathematical expectations of the future can be formulated.

Needless to say, it is very challenging to predict the market direction of any financial market. The further out the time horizon, the less reliable the forecast. That's why I have limited VantagePoint's forecasts to four trading days, which is more than enough lead time to gain a tremendous trading advantage.

Trying to predict crude oil or the S&P 500 Index a month, six months or a year from now is impractical from a trading standpoint. This is due in part to the fact that market dynamics entail both randomness and unforeseen events that are, by definition, unpredictable. Plus, let's face it, forecasting is not an exact science; there's a lot of "art" involved.

I have successfully applied neural networks to intermarket data in order to forecast moving averages, turning them into a *leading indicator* that pinpoints expected changes in market trend direction with nearly 80% accuracy. This is in sharp contrast to using moving averages as a *lagging indicator*, as most traders still do, to determine where the trend has been.

> **I have successfully applied neural networks to inter-market data in order to forecast moving averages, turning them into a *leading indicator* that pinpoints expected changes in market trend direction with nearly 80% accuracy.**

If you are driving down an interstate highway at seventy miles per hour, you wouldn't only look backwards through your rear window or over your shoulder. You need to look forward, out the front window at the road ahead, so you can anticipate possible dangers in order to prevent an accident from happening. It is the same with trading.

An enormous competitive advantage is realized by being able to anticipate future price action, even by just a day or two, so you can guide your trading decisions based upon your expectation of what is about to happen.

VantagePoint uses price, volume and open interest data on each target futures market and selected related markets as inputs into its neural networks. In this manner, its moving average forecasts are not based solely upon single-market price inputs.

In the case of VantagePoint's Nasdaq-100® program, for example, the raw inputs into the forecast of the moving averages include the daily open, high, low, close, volume and open interest for the Nasdaq-100 Index, plus nine related markets as shown in Figure 4-5.

**Figure 4-5. INTERMARKET DATA USED BY VANTAGEPOINT'S NASDAQ-100 PROGRAM**

- Dow Jones Industrial Average
- 30-Year Treasury Bonds
- S&P 500 Index
- U.S. Dollar Index
- S&P 100®

- NYSE Composite Index®
- Bridge/CRB Index
- Dow Jones Utility Average℠
- Light Crude Oil

**VantagePoint's Nasdaq-100 program analyzes the Nasdaq-100 Index plus nine related markets to generate intermarket-based forecasts.**

Source: Market Technologies Corporation

Similarly, every other VantagePoint program has its own specific related markets, which provide intermarket input data into its neural networks.

# Leading Indicators Give You a Competitive Edge

Since identifying the trend direction of a market is so critical to successful trading of that market, *trend forecasting* strategies offer a substantial competitive advantage over traditional market lagging, *trend following* strategies.

I have found that predicted moving averages are most effective for trend forecasting when they are incorporated into more complex indicators, such as moving average crossover strategies, which can be used to identify not only the anticipated direction of the trend but also its strength. This has been implemented within VantagePoint by comparing predicted moving averages for certain time periods in the future with today's actual moving averages of the same length.

For instance, VantagePoint compares a predicted 10-day moving average for four days in the future with today's actual 10-day moving average calculated as of today's close. It also forecasts other moving averages and makes similar comparisons, including that of a predicted 5-day moving average for two days in the future with today's actual 5-day moving average calculated through today's close.

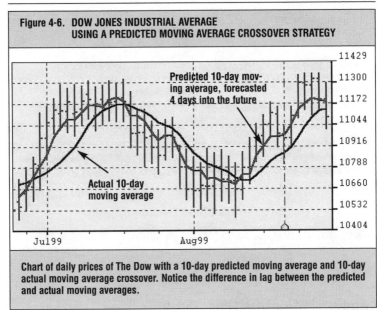

**Figure 4-6. DOW JONES INDUSTRIAL AVERAGE USING A PREDICTED MOVING AVERAGE CROSSOVER STRATEGY**

Predicted 10-day moving average, forecasted 4 days into the future

Actual 10-day moving average

Jul99    Aug99

Chart of daily prices of The Dow with a 10-day predicted moving average and 10-day actual moving average crossover. Notice the difference in lag between the predicted and actual moving averages.

Source: VantagePoint Intermarket Analysis Software

Figure 4-6 shows a crossover of the predicted 10-day moving average and the actual 10-day moving average for the Dow Jones Industrial Average. Notice that the predicted moving average, because it is being forecasted for four days in advance, does not lag behind the market, while the actual 10-day moving average lags behind both the market and the predicted moving average.

The leading indicators within VantagePoint, involving the crossover of predicted moving averages with actual moving averages, will be discussed in more detail in the next chapter.

*Chapter 5*

# VANTAGEPOINT FORECASTS MARKET DIRECTION

## How to Get a Sneak Preview of Where the Markets Are Going and Use This Information to Your Advantage

VantagePoint uses the pattern recognition capabilities of neural networks to analyze market data from each target market plus selected related markets in order to make forecasts for that target market. This is accomplished by predicting short-term moving averages, which are then used to indicate the market direction of each target market.

Since 1991 when VantagePoint was first introduced, Market Technologies Corporation's research team, the Predictive Technologies Group, under my direction has continued to conduct proprietary research and development with neural networks and intermarket analysis. Updated versions of VantagePoint have been released as improvements in its forecasting accuracy have been achieved.

## VantagePoint Monitors Major Financial Markets

Presently there are twenty-five actively traded financial markets that VantagePoint monitors each day. These include interest rates, stock indexes, energies and currencies, as presented in Figure 5-1 on page 72.

With its ability to make consistently accurate trend forecasts for these actively traded financial markets, VantagePoint offers a competitive advantage, from an intermarket perspective, to serious traders in the futures, options and equity markets. It's not a crystal ball, but it may be the next best thing.

Many VantagePoint clients day trade while others position trade or do a combination of both. Some clients trade full-time while others, employed outside the financial industry, trade part-time.

Typically VantagePoint is used by traders in conjunction with other technical trading tools that they are already using. In this way VantagePoint's predictive indicators act as intermarket confirmation filters to various single-market indicators that only look internally at each market.

When VantagePoint confirms these single-market indicators from an intermarket perspective, that's a green light to take the trade. However, when VantagePoint is in disagreement with these single-market indicators, that's a bright yellow *caution* light.

---

**FIGURE 5-1. FINANCIAL MARKETS COVERED BY VANTAGEPOINT**

| INTEREST RATES | STOCK INDEXES |
|---|---|
| 30-Year T-Bonds | S&P 500 |
| 10-Year T-Notes | S&P 100 |
| 5-Year T-Notes | FTSE 100 |
| 2-Year T-Notes | Nikkei |
| Eurodollar | Nasdaq-100 |
| | Nasdaq Composite |
| | Dow |

| ENERGIES | CURRENCIES |
|---|---|
| Gasoline | Swiss Franc |
| Natural Gas | Deutsche Mark |
| Gas Oil | British Pound |
| Brent Crude | Canadian Dollar |
| Light Crude | Australian Dollar |
| Heating Oil | U.S. Dollar Index |
| | Japanese Yen |

VantagePoint monitors interest rate, stock index, energy and currency markets, giving intermarket-based forecasts.

Source: Market Technologies Corporation

After spending a little time becoming familiar at first with its reports and charts, it takes just a few minutes each day to update Vantage-Point and have its predictive intermarket-based information available for making your trading decisions.

Figure 5-2 lists the predictive accuracy of VantagePoint's trend forecasts, based on its proprietary Neural Index indicator (which will be discussed later), for each of the twenty-five financial markets currently monitored by VantagePoint.

# Five Neural Networks Make Independent Forecasts

Each VantagePoint program is specifically designed for a particular target market and uses five neural networks, in a two-level hierarchy, to forecast five different leading indicators for that market.

- The first network forecasts tomorrow's High, to help set stops for entry and exit points.

- The second network forecasts tomorrow's Low, to help set stops for entry and exit points.

- The third network forecasts a 5-day moving average of closes for two days in the future, to indicate the expected Short-Term trend direction within the next two days.

- The fourth network forecasts a 10-day moving average of closes for four days in the future, to indicate the expected Medium-Term trend direction within the next four days.

- The fifth network indicates if the market is expected to change trend direction by making a *top* or *bottom* within the next two days.

> **While the underlying mathematics behind Vantage-Point is very complex, its forecasted intermarket-based trading information is easy to understand.**

The first four networks at the primary level of the network hierarchy make independent market forecasts of the High, Low, Short-Term trend and Medium-Term trend. These forecasts are then used as inputs into the fifth network along with other target market and intermarket data inputs, at the secondary level of the network hierarchy, to predict market Turning Points. VantagePoint's neural network configuration is shown in Figure 5-3 (see page 75).

While the underlying mathematics behind VantagePoint is very complex, its forecasted intermarket-based trading information is easy to understand. Even a new trader with no background in mathematics or technical analysis can begin to benefit immediately from its information. VantagePoint is designed for active traders, not engineers or rocket scientists.

VantagePoint's forecasts are presented for each target market in a one-page Daily Report. A more detailed History Report is also available for more in-depth analysis. VantagePoint's predictive information is also exportable to other software programs. Additionally, all of the indicators presented in the Daily Report can be displayed or printed as detailed color charts, for traders who are more visually oriented.

Figure 5-4 (see page 76) shows a VantagePoint chart of the Dow Jones Industrial Average with its predicted 10-day moving average

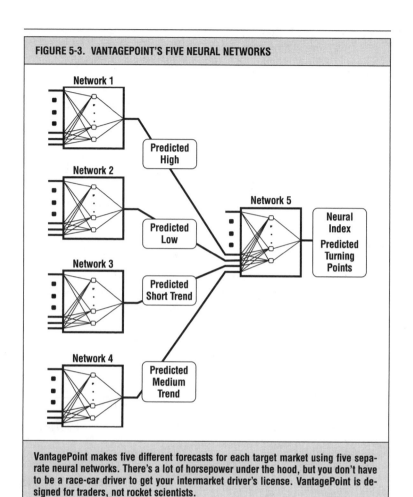

**FIGURE 5-3. VANTAGEPOINT'S FIVE NEURAL NETWORKS**

Network 1

Predicted High

Network 2

Predicted Low

Network 5

Neural Index
Predicted Turning Points

Network 3

Predicted Short Trend

Network 4

Predicted Medium Trend

VantagePoint makes five different forecasts for each target market using five separate neural networks. There's a lot of horsepower under the hood, but you don't have to be a race-car driver to get your intermarket driver's license. VantagePoint is designed for traders, not rocket scientists.

Source: Market Technologies Corporation

and actual 10-day moving average superimposed on the daily prices. In this example, the entry point to go long occurs when the predicted moving average crosses the actual moving average from below to above as indicated by the "up arrow" at the left of the chart. The long position is maintained until the predicted moving average crosses the actual moving average from above to below as indicated by the "down arrow" at the right of the chart.

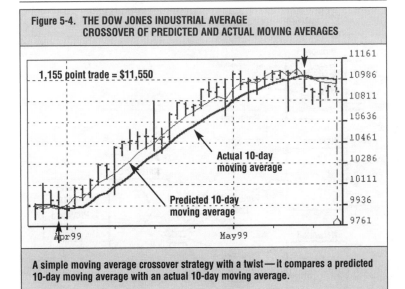

Figure 5-4. THE DOW JONES INDUSTRIAL AVERAGE
CROSSOVER OF PREDICTED AND ACTUAL MOVING AVERAGES

1,155 point trade = $11,550

Actual 10-day
moving average

Predicted 10-day
moving average

A simple moving average crossover strategy with a twist—it compares a predicted
10-day moving average with an actual 10-day moving average.

Source: VantagePoint Intermarket Analysis Software

Figure 5-5 (see page 77) shows a sample VantagePoint Daily Report for the Nasdaq Composite Index. Notice that the report is divided into three sections, each of which will be discussed in detail shortly.

Figure 5-6 (see page 77) shows a sample VantagePoint History Report for the Nasdaq Composite Index.

The layout, information and interpretation of a VantagePoint chart or report for one target market are identical to those for each of the other target markets. Therefore, once you are familiar using Vantage-Point on one market, it is simple to use it on others. In fact, Vantage-Point is designed so that it can be updated on all twenty-five markets automatically at the touch of your mouse button. The whole process takes just a few minutes each day.

## What VantagePoint's Daily Report Tells You

Each Daily Report gives you intermarket-based forecasts for use on the next trading day, in addition to information from previous days to give some background on what has just happened in that market.

Figure 5-7 displays Section 1 of a VantagePoint Daily Report for the 10-year Treasury notes program.

**Section 1** displays the following information:

- Today's *actual* Open, High, Low, Close.
- Today's *actual* 5-day simple moving average of closes. This is labeled TrndS (for Trend Short).
- Today's *actual* 10-day simple moving average of closes. This is labeled TrndM (for Trend Medium).

Figure 5-8 (see page 79) displays Section 2 of a VantagePoint Daily Report for the 10-year Treasury notes program.

**Section 2** displays the following information:

- Tomorrow's *predicted* High. This is labeled PHigh.
- Tomorrow's *predicted* Low. This is labeled PLow.
- *Predicted* 5-day simple moving average of closes *for two days in the future*. This is labeled PTS (for Predicted Trend Short). Three of the closing prices (today, yesterday and the day before yesterday) are

---

**FIGURE 5-7. 10-YEAR TREASURY NOTES — SECTION 1 OF THE DAILY REPORT**

**VantagePoint Daily Report**
10-Year T-Note

|  | Open | High | Low | Close | TrndS | TrndM |
|---|---|---|---|---|---|---|
| 4/24/00 | 9816 | 9840 | 9812 | 9816 | 9806 | 9819 |
| 4/25/00 | 9816 | 9816 | 9732 | 9734 | 9802 | 9808 |
| 4/26/00 | 9732 | 9754 | 9730 | 9736 | 9763 | 9802 |
| 4/27/00 | 9734 | 9748 | 9646 | 9654 | 9744 | 9759 |
| 4/28/00 | 9656 | 9712 | 9630 | 9662 | 9728 | 9750 |
| 5/01/00 | 9660 | 9702 | 9644 | 9646 | 9708 | 9739 |
| 5/02/00 | 9646 | 9656 | 9626 | 9628 | 9658 | 9730 |
| 5/03/00 | 9626 | 9638 | 9558 | 9562 | 9638 | 9718 |
| 5/04/00 | 9600 | 9608 | 9532 | 9536 | 9621 | 9701 |
| 5/05/00 | 9540 | 9562 | 9512 | 9518 | 9600 | 9646 |
| 5/08/00 | 9518 | 9534 | 9460 | 9500 | 9542 | 9625 |
| 5/09/00 | 9460 | 9520 | 9456 | 9516 | (9526) | (9610) |

Actual 5-day ↗
moving average

Actual 10-day ↑
moving average

Section 1 of the Daily Report displays the Open, High, Low, Close, actual 5-day and actual 10-day moving average.

Source: VantagePoint Intermarket Analysis Software

FIGURE 5-8. 10-YEAR TREASURY NOTES—SECTION 2 OF THE DAILY REPORT

**VantagePoint Daily Report**
10-Year T-Note

| | PHigh | PLow | PTS | PTM |
|---|---|---|---|---|
| 4/24/00 | 9829 | 9800 | 9812 | 9816 |
| 4/25/00 | 9747 | 9712 | 9752 | 9751 |
| 4/26/00 | 9755 | 9724 | 9743 | 9748 |
| 4/27/00 | 9704 | 9630 | 9710 | 9725 |
| 4/28/00 | 9723 | 9646 | 9701 | 9723 |
| 5/01/00 | 9703 | 9632 | 9650 | 9701 |
| 5/02/00 | 9645 | 9616 | 9640 | 9652 |
| 5/03/00 | 9612 | 9543 | 9614 | 9637 |
| 5/04/00 | 9550 | 9518 | 9554 | 9619 |
| 5/05/00 | 9533 | 9502 | 9531 | 9601 |
| 5/08/00 | 9519 | 9448 | 9513 | 9546 |
| 5/09/00 | 9535 | 9462 | 9512 | 9537 |

Predicted trading range for the next day

Predicted 5-day moving average

Predicted 10-day moving average

Section 2 of the Daily Report displays the predicted High, predicted Low, predicted 5-day moving average and predicted 10-day moving average.

Source: VantagePoint Intermarket Analysis Software

known since they have already occurred up through today's close. The remaining two closing prices (for tomorrow and the day after tomorrow) are not known since they have not yet occurred.

- *Predicted* 10-day simple moving average of closes *for four days in the future.* This is labeled PTM (for Predicted Trend Medium), in which six of the closing prices are known, but the remaining four closing prices are not known.

Figure 5-9 (see page 80) displays Section 3 of a VantagePoint Daily Report for the 10-year Treasury notes program.

**Section 3** displays the following information:

- The *Strength Index*, a weighted composite of the four indicators from Section 2, indicates if the market is getting overbought or oversold.
- *PHigh Diff* displays the difference between the predicted High for tomorrow from Section 2, and today's actual High from Section 1.
- *PLow Diff* displays the difference between the predicted Low for tomorrow from Section 2, and today's actual Low from Section 1.

Trend Forecasting With Technical Analysis     **79**

**VantagePoint Daily Report**
10-Year T-Note

| | Strength | PHighDiff | PLowDiff | Index | PTSDiff | PTMDiff |
|---|---|---|---|---|---|---|
| 4/24/00 | -0.36 | -11 | -12 | 1.00 | 6 | -3 |
| 4/25/00 | -0.70 | -33 | -20 | 0.00 | -14 | -21 |
| 4/26/00 | -0.45 | 1 | -6 | 0.00 | -20 | -18 |
| 4/27/00 | -0.73 | -44 | -16 | 0.00 | -34 | -34 |
| 4/28/00 | 0.15 | 11 | 16 | 0.00 | -27 | -27 |
| 5/01/00 | -0.50 | 1 | -12 | 0.00 | -22 | -38 |
| 5/02/00 | -0.69 | -11 | -10 | 0.00 | -18 | -42 |
| 5/03/00 | -0.72 | -26 | -15 | 0.00 | -24 | -45 |
| 5/04/00 | -0.72 | -22 | -14 | 0.00 | -31 | -46 |
| 5/05/00 | -0.72 | -29 | -10 | 0.00 | -33 | -45 |
| 5/08/00 | -0.71 | -15 | -12 | 0.00 | -29 | -43 |
| 5/09/00 | 0.09 | 15 | 6 | 0.00 | -14 | -37 |

Index turns to 0.00
indicating weakness

PTS Diff becomes negative indicating weakness

PTM Diff becomes
more negative
indicating further
weakness

Section 3 of the Daily Report displays the Strength Index, differences between the predicted indicators and today's actual indicators, and the Neural Index. This section alerts you to an impending change in market direction and strength.

Source: VantagePoint Intermarket Analysis Software

- The *Neural Index* indicates whether or not the market is expected to make a *top* or *bottom* and change trend direction within the next two days, based on a comparison of two 3-day moving averages.

- *PTS Diff* displays the difference between the predicted 5-day moving average for two days in the future (PTS) from Section 2, and today's actual 5-day moving average (TrndS) from Section 1.

- *PTM Diff* displays the difference between the predicted 10-day moving average for four days in the future (PTM) from Section 2, and today's actual 10-day moving average (TrndM) from Section 1.

# Intermarket Charts Show You What's Ahead

VantagePoint has extensive charting capabilities to help you visualize its forecasts of market trend direction and prices. This is really what makes VantagePoint so unique.

Unlike traditional charts, VantagePoint's charts show you where it expects the market to go next, not just where it has been in the past.

While other traders are still relying solely upon single-market trend following indicators, which look *backward* and can only identify trend changes *after* the fact, VantagePoint lets you look *forward* so you get a sneak preview of what's ahead. This is like having a road map that other traders can't decipher because they don't know the secret code.

VantagePoint has two modes of chart presentation: Overlay and Displaced.

• In Overlay mode, the predicted indicator is plotted on the day that the prediction is made.

• In Displaced mode, the indicator is plotted on the day for which it is predicted rather than on the day the prediction is made.

Figure 5-10 displays a VantagePoint chart showing the predicted 10-day moving average of the 10-year Treasury notes plotted in Overlay mode. This indicator predicts what the 10-day moving average value will be four days in the future. Notice how turns in the predicted moving average do not lag behind turns in the market itself.

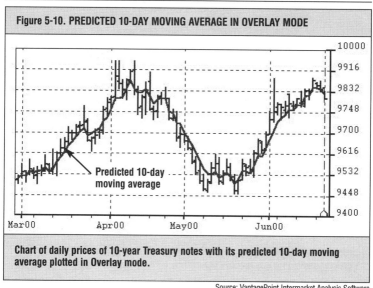

**Figure 5-10. PREDICTED 10-DAY MOVING AVERAGE IN OVERLAY MODE**

Chart of daily prices of 10-year Treasury notes with its predicted 10-day moving average plotted in Overlay mode.

Source: VantagePoint Intermarket Analysis Software

Figure 5-11 displays a VantagePoint chart showing the next day's predicted High and Low of the Dow Jones Industrial Average plotted in Displaced mode onto the actual day that corresponds to the predictions. These price forecasts are used by traders to determine entry and exit points, which will be discussed later in this chapter.

## VantagePoint Is Quick and Easy

Each evening after the markets close, that day's open, high, low, close, volume and open interest data on each target market and its nine related markets are downloaded from a VantagePoint-compatible data vendor's database or over the Internet. When you perform the Daily Update function within VantagePoint this information is automatically processed by VantagePoint's five neural networks which then generate their forecasts for the next day's trading.

All you have to do is compare the Daily Reports (or charts) for several target markets to one another, to see which markets offer the best trades to take the next day. The process takes only a few minutes from start to finish. If there is not a clear-cut indication of market direction, you would pass on taking a trade in that particular market.

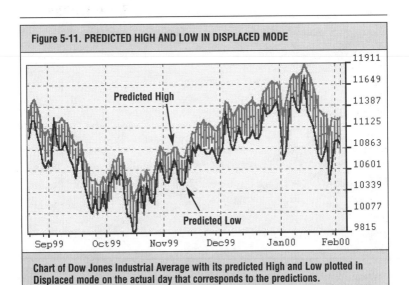

**Figure 5-11. PREDICTED HIGH AND LOW IN DISPLACED MODE**

Chart of Dow Jones Industrial Average with its predicted High and Low plotted in Displaced mode on the actual day that corresponds to the predictions.

Source: VantagePoint Intermarket Analysis Software

Only those trades with the highest probability of success should be taken. This stacks the odds in your favor.

Let's look at the steps to follow in determining whether or not a trade is worth taking.

## How to Find a Good Trade

The Neural Index in Section 3 of the Daily Report is a good place to start to get an indication of the expected market trend direction. The Neural Index is a proprietary indicator, determined by comparing two 3-day moving averages to one another:

- Today's *actual* 3-day moving average, which is the sum of today's close ($Day_t$), yesterday's close ($Day_{t-1}$) and the close of the day prior to yesterday's close ($Day_{t-2}$) divided by 3.

- A *predicted* 3-day moving average, which is the sum of today's close ($Day_t$), tomorrow's close ($Day_{t+1}$) and the close of the day after tomorrow ($Day_{t+2}$) divided by 3.

The forecast of the predicted 3-day moving average is made by Vantage-Point's fifth neural network, using predictions from the other four networks as inputs, in addition to data from the target market itself and the specific related markets pertaining to that target market.

> **The Neural Index in Section 3 of the Daily Report is a good place to start to get an indication of the expected market trend direction. The Neural Index is a proprietary indicator, determined by comparing two 3-day moving averages to one another.**

When the predicted 3-day moving average value is greater than today's actual 3-day moving average value, the Neural Index is 1.00. This indicates that VantagePoint expects the market to move *higher* over the next two days.

When the predicted 3-day moving average value is less than today's actual 3-day moving average value, the Neural Index is 0.00. This indicates that the market is expected to move *lower* over the next two days.

With an overall predictive accuracy rate of nearly 80% as indicated in Figure 5-2 (see page 73), the Neural Index will give you added confidence to pull the trigger when there is a strong indication that a market is about to make a *top* or *bottom* and poised to change trend direction.

## Here's How to Get Added Confirmation

You can use the PTS Diff and the PTM Diff indicators in Section 3 of the Daily Report in conjunction with the Neural Index to confirm the expected market direction. The strongest confirmation occurs when the Index, PTS Diff and PTM Diff are in agreement with each other.

Each day as VantagePoint's neural networks are updated with the most recent data on the target market and its related markets, VantagePoint makes its forecasts and calculates the difference in value between each predicted moving average and the actual moving average of the same length. By using forecasted moving averages, VantagePoint retains all of the smoothing effects of moving averages, while effectively eliminating the lag.

When the predicted moving average crosses *above* the actual moving average (the PTS Diff or PTM Diff turns *positive*), VantagePoint expects the market trend to turn *up* within the forecast time horizon related to each of these two indicators.

- When the PTS Diff is positive, reaches a maximum positive value and narrows (indicating that the upward trend is beginning to lose strength), this gives you an early warning that the market is about to make a *top* and turn down within the next two days.

- When the PTM Diff is positive, reaches a maximum positive value and narrows (indicating that the upward trend is beginning to lose strength), this gives you an early warning that the market is about to make a *top* and turn down within the next four days.

Similarly, when the predicted moving average crosses *below* the actual moving average (the PTS Diff or PTM Diff turns *negative*), VantagePoint expects the market trend to turn *down* within the forecast time horizon related to each of these two indicators.

- When the PTS Diff is negative, reaches a maximum negative value and narrows (indicating that the downward trend is beginning to lose strength), this gives you an early warning that the market is about to make a *bottom* and turn up within the next two days.

- When the PTM Diff is negative, reaches a maximum negative value and narrows (indicating that the downward trend is beginning to lose strength), this gives you an early warning that the market is about to make a *bottom* and turn up within the next four days.

Rather than wait for the crossover to actually occur, you can make trading decisions based on the narrowing in the PTS Diff or PTM Diff, which is the earliest warning that the market trend is beginning to lose strength. For instance, if you are in a long position, you can act on this information in a number of ways depending on your account size, risk propensity, information derived from single-market technical indicators that you also utilize, your trading style and objectives. Here are just three possible strategies that can be implemented:

> You can use the PTS Diff and the PTM Diff indicators in Section 3 of the Daily Report in conjunction with the Neural Index to confirm the expected market direction. The strongest confirmation occurs when the Index, PTS Diff and PTM Diff are in agreement with each other.

- If the PTS Diff or PTM Diff reaches a maximum positive value and narrows by even a small amount, you can close out your long position and stand aside. Then you can wait for either the PTS Diff or PTM Diff to narrow further or wait for one or both of them to turn negative before taking a short trade, even if the Neural Index has still not changed to 0.00. If either the PTS Diff or PTM Diff (or both) instead show renewed strength (the difference between the predicted and the actual moving average value widens again instead of continues to narrow), you could re-enter your long position.

- If the PTS Diff or PTM Diff reaches a maximum positive value and narrows by even a small amount and the Index is 1.00, you can tighten your stop and stay in your long position. With this strategy you are still long should the market show renewed strength. If, instead, the difference continues to narrow on subsequent days, you would close out your long position and stand aside or reverse positions.

- If the PTS Diff or PTM Diff reaches a maximum positive value and narrows by a predetermined minimum amount, you can close out your long position and go short, even if the Index has still not changed to 0.00. This strategy is the most aggressive of the three since it involves reversing positions at the earliest indication that the current market trend is likely to make a top and change direction.

Likewise, if you are short you would wait for the PTS Diff or PTM Diff to reach a maximum negative value and narrow before following one of these three strategies.

To the extent that the PTS Diff and PTM Diff behave similar to each other from one day to the next (and are confirmed by the Neural Index), you can be more confident that the market will move as expected within the forecast time horizons of these three indicators.

By creating trend forecasting strategies, which compare predicted moving averages with actual moving averages, you can get an early warning of an impending change in trend direction—days before it would show up on a traditional price chart or be identified by single-market trend following indicators such as lagging moving average crossover approaches.

## Here's a Simple Example

Figure 5-12 is an example of a 10-year Treasury notes trade. In practice, each day after you update Vantage-Point you would see the latest Index, PTS Diff and PTM Diff values in Section 3 of that day's Daily Report.

For the purpose of this example, the more conservative trading strategy of waiting for the Index to change from 1.00 to 0.00, and for the PTS Diff and PTM Diff to both turn negative before entering a short trade will be examined. Therefore the following relatively stringent conditions, which indicate that the market is likely to make a top and that weakness is about to set in, will need to be met:

**Figure 5-12. VANTAGEPOINT PREDICTS A MARKET TOP AS MARKET SHOWS STRENGTH**

|  | Index | PTS Diff | PTM Diff |
|---|---|---|---|
| 4/24/00 | 1.00 | 6 | -3 |
| 4/25/00 | 0.00 | -14 | -21 |
| 4/26/00 | 0.00 | -20 | -18 |
| 4/27/00 | 0.00 | -34 | -34 |
| 4/28/00 | 0.00 | -27 | -27 |

Changes in the Index, PTS Diff and PTM Diff over a five-day period warn that the market is about to make a top and turn down.

Source: Market Technologies Corporation

- If the Index value is 1.00 indicating that the market is in an *up* trend, you would wait for the Index to change to 0.00.

- If the PTS Diff is positive indicating that the market is in an *up* trend, you would wait for the PTS Diff to narrow and turn negative.

- If the PTM Diff is positive indicating that the market is in an *up* trend, you would wait for the PTM Diff to narrow and turn negative.

After the close on 4/24/00 VantagePoint reported an Index value of 1.00, a PTS Diff of 6, and a PTM Diff of –3. While the market showed strength, with progressively higher highs and higher lows on 4/19/00, 4/20/00 and 4/24/00, the negative PTM Diff on 4/24/00 is the first clear cut confirmation that the market is expected to weaken and turn down.

After the close on 4/25/00, the Index changed from 1.00 to 0.00 and the PTS Diff changed from 6 to –14, confirming the weakness that was indicated on 4/24/00 by the negative PTM Diff. In fact, on 4/25/00 the PTM Diff indicated even further expected weakness, as it changed from –3 to –21. When these three leading indicators confirm each other like this, it is a strong indication that a short position can be taken. The expectation of impending weakness was reaffirmed after the close on 4/26/00, when the Index remained at 0.00 and the PTS Diff changed from –14 to –20.

> **By creating trend forecasting strategies, which compare predicted moving averages with actual moving averages, you can get an early warning of an impending change in trend direction.**

Once the Index changes from 1.00 to 0.00 and the PTS Diff and PTM Diff change from positive to negative, further weakness is indicated on subsequent days if the Index remains at 0.00 and the PTS Diff and PTM Diff become even more negative. This is what happened after the close on 4/27/00, when the Index remained at 0.00 and both the PTS Diff and PTM Diff changed to -34 in value.

The opposite scenario suggests taking a long position. This happens when the Index changes from 0.00 to 1.00 and the PTS Diff and PTM Diff are negative and start to narrow by getting less negative, before changing to positive values. For even more confirmation, the Strength Index can be used to determine the extent to which the market is getting overbought (large positive values) or oversold (large negative values).

# Day and Position Trading With Tomorrow's Price Forecasts

Once you have identified the expected trend direction using the Index, PTS Diff and PTM Diff from Section 3 of the Daily Report, you can set your entry point, by looking at the next day's predicted High and predicted Low in Section 2 of the Daily Report. These price forecasts create an expected trading range for the next day, which is analogous to extending support and resistance lines in traditional single-market technical analysis approaches.

The advantage of VantagePoint, though, is that the next day's High and Low forecasts, based on the pattern recognition capabilities of neural networks applied to intermarket data, are objectively determined and are not just an arbitrary linear extrapolation from past single-market data.

If you are a day trader, you can use the forecasts of the next day's High and Low to identify low-risk day trades. If the Neural Index and forecasted moving average indicators for a specific target market indicate that the next day is expected to be a *down* day, you can wait for the market to trade up toward the predicted High before initiating a short position with a limit or market order, with the intention of closing out the trade near the predicted Low.

The left side of Figure 5-13 (see page 89) displays the forecast made after the close on 4/25/00 for the High on 4/26/00 to be 9747 for 10-year Treasury notes. VantagePoint also forecasted this market to go *down* on 4/26/00, indicating that day traders can enter short positions near the predicted High. The right side of Figure 5-13 shows what actually happened on 4/26/00.

Similarly, long positions can be entered near the predicted Low on a day expected to be *up*, with exits near the predicted High. This allows day traders to sell rallies within an expected downtrend or buy dips within an expected uptrend, one or more times daily depending on the intraday market volatility. The profitability of day trades that are executed with this strategy can be substantial with minimal risk, since tight stops can be utilized.

If you are a position trader, you can use the forecasts of the next day's High and Low to enter positions, then use the subsequent days' forecasts to move your stop or exit the trade. For example, let's say

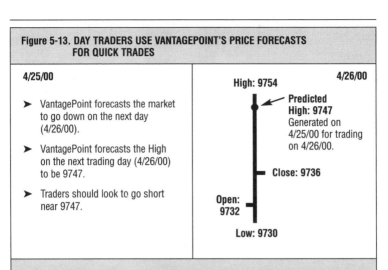

**Figure 5-13. DAY TRADERS USE VANTAGEPOINT'S PRICE FORECASTS FOR QUICK TRADES**

**4/25/00**

➤ VantagePoint forecasts the market to go down on the next day (4/26/00).

➤ VantagePoint forecasts the High on the next trading day (4/26/00) to be 9747.

➤ Traders should look to go short near 9747.

**4/26/00**

High: 9754

Predicted High: 9747 Generated on 4/25/00 for trading on 4/26/00.

Close: 9736

Open: 9732

Low: 9730

VantagePoint forecasts this market to go down on 4/26/00. Day traders can enter a short position near the predicted High of 9747, covering the short before the end of the day.

Source: Market Technologies Corporation

it's 4/25/00 and you just looked at tonight's Daily Report and everything indicates a bearish bias for the next day. You decide you want to go short on 4/26/00. You can determine where you should enter the market by looking at the predicted High for 4/26/00, as shown on the Daily Report of 4/25/00 in Figure 5-14. In this case you could enter a short position at or near 9747.

**Figure 5-14. PREDICTED HIGH AND LOW IN SECTION 2**

|  | PHigh | PLow |
|---|---|---|
| 4/25/00 | 9747 | 9712 |

Position traders can enter short positions near the predicted High, and stay in the position until the market is expected to make a bottom.

Source: Market Technologies Corporation

# Stop Placement Based on Forecasts Not Hunches

You could put a protective buy stop somewhere above the predicted High of 9747 depending on your risk propensity so your stop is sufficiently outside of the daily range that VantagePoint forecasts for 4/26/00. This would lessen the probability of being stopped out prematurely due to intraday market volatility, yet protect you in the event the market penetrates the predicted High and breaks out to the upside.

The benefit of setting your stop based on forecasts of the next day's High or Low is that your stop is less likely to be clustered among other traders' stops which are typically set through traditional methods of single-market analysis such as extending support and resistance trend lines.

As a position trader you would stay in your short position until the following day. Then if VantagePoint indicates continued expected weakness on the Daily Report updated after the close of 4/26/00 (to be used for trading on 4/27/00), you would hold the short position for another day. In this case the market opened at 9734 on 4/27/00 and ended up closing substantially lower at 9654 as shown previously in Figure 5-7 (see page 78). In fact, from Figure 5-9 (see page 80) you can see that the Index, PTS Diff and PTM Diff all indicated sustained weakness through 5/8/00 as Treasury notes moved lower by nearly three points.

## Other Markets Give Added Confirmation

Since the neural networks for each VantagePoint program have been developed and trained independently for each particular target market, daily reports from other target markets can be used for additional confirmation.

Once you are familiar with one Daily Report, and understand what to look for in terms of the PHigh, PLow, Neural Index, PTS Diff and PTM Diff, it is simple to understand the Daily Reports for other markets monitored by VantagePoint.

The eurodollar, 2-year Treasury notes, 5-year Treasury notes and the 30-year Treasury bonds daily reports, for example, add considerable insight into what is likely to happen to 10-year Treasury notes, since these five markets taken together encompass the entire interest rate yield curve from ninety days to thirty years.

The more the forecasted indicators on these other reports confirm the indicators on the 10-year Treasury notes Daily Report, the higher the probability that the Treasury notes market will act as expected. On the other hand, if these other reports give contrary indications, you should be cautious. Similar confirmations or divergences can be found among the energy markets, stock indexes and currencies monitored by VantagePoint.

Even traders who do not trade futures but only buy and sell individual stocks (such as new economy technology stocks comprising the Nasdaq Composite Index or old economy stocks comprising The Dow) can use VantagePoint's Nasdaq and Dow programs for timing individual stock transactions.

## How To "Cherry-Pick" the Best Trades to Take

With VantagePoint programs covering major financial markets, traders with multiple programs can pick only those trades to take each day that have the highest probability of being profitable. I call this "cherry-picking." This lets you avoid the trap that many other traders fall into, in which they feel compelled to trade even when there isn't a good trade to be taken. So they chase after marginal trades, with predictably negative results.

If you can appreciate the advantage of having intermarket-based trend forecasts with nearly 80% accuracy at predicting short-term market direction, and the benefit of broadening your perspective of the markets beyond simply focusing on the internal dynamics within each individual market, then you will become a believer in intermarket analysis and the power of neural networks as a market forecasting tool.

In the next chapter I will explain very briefly in non-mathematical terms what neural networks are and how they can be utilized as a forecasting tool to predict the market direction of any financial market.

# Chapter 6

# NEURAL NETWORKS
## How to Raise Your Financial IQ to Stay Ahead of the Competition

The human brain is composed of hundreds of billions of cells known as neurons, which through their connections to each other relay information from one neuron to another. This process allows a person to learn relationships, draw inferences, recognize patterns and make predictions, among other tasks. While substantially less complex than the human brain, neural networks model how it processes information and performs pattern recognition and forecasting.

Neural networks are comprised of individual neurons organized in layers and interconnected through network architecture with variable mathematical weights attributed to each connection. The architecture includes an input layer, hidden layer and an output layer.

Neural networks are excellent at sifting through enormous amounts of seemingly unrelated market data and finding repetitive patterns that could never be perceived visually just by looking at

> **Neural networks are excellent at sifting through enormous amounts of seemingly unrelated market data and finding repetitive patterns that could never be perceived visually just by looking at price charts or by comparing two markets to one another.**

price charts or by comparing two markets to one another. Through a mathematical error minimization process known as "learning" or "training," neural networks, if designed properly, can be trained to make highly accurate market forecasts based upon these patterns.

# Neural Networks Combine Technical and Intermarket Data

VantagePoint's neural networks are designed and trained to make specific forecasts for each target market. The raw input data from the target market and related markets, statistical "preprocessing" of the raw data, network architecture, as well as the training and testing regimens are tailored to each target market.

Figure 6-1 depicts how single-market technical data from a target market and intermarket data from related markets are fed into VantagePoint's neural networks to make predictions for each of the twenty-five target markets that VantagePoint monitors each day.

Like back-testing and optimization a decade earlier, neural networks at first had their skeptics and detractors in the financial industry in the early 1990s, around the time the first version of VantagePoint was released. Software developers from outside of the financial industry, knowledgeable about neural networks applied to other arenas and perceiving a potentially lucrative marketplace for their software among traders, flooded into the financial industry offering an assortment of neural network software programs to traders. Before long neural networks were being hyped in promotional marketing literature as the Holy Grail of technical analysis as expectations about their potential reached dizzying heights.

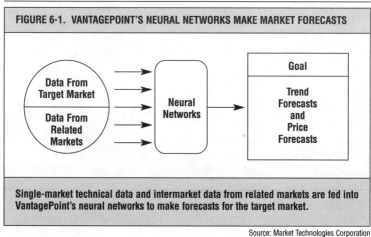

**FIGURE 6-1. VANTAGEPOINT'S NEURAL NETWORKS MAKE MARKET FORECASTS**

Data From Target Market

Data From Related Markets

Neural Networks

Goal

Trend Forecasts and Price Forecasts

Single-market technical data and intermarket data from related markets are fed into VantagePoint's neural networks to make forecasts for the target market.

Unfamiliar with the intricacies of the financial markets and the details underlying technical analysis, many of these newcomers to the financial industry helped foster a backlash against neural networks among traders as the Holy Grail remained elusive.

My focus, though, since the mid-1980s has been intermarket analysis. Neural networks just happen to be the best mathematical tool that I have identified for finding hidden patterns and relationships in seemingly disparate market data and making highly accurate short-term market forecasts in a non-subjective, quantitative manner. Neural networks are not a magic bullet. They are the means, not the end.

# Neural Networks Learn Patterns and Make Forecasts

Over the past decade since first appearing on the financial industry scene, neural networks have been applied successfully to financial forecasting, corporate decision-making (including risk analysis and fraud detection), character recognition and medical diagnostics, to name a few application areas.

Recently with prominent software companies developing and promoting neural network software for decision analysis such as Computer Associates International's Neugents™ software, neural networks have become more accepted as a mainstream mathematical tool.

## The Input Layer

A neural network is not limited to single-market technical data inputs. A neural network is excellent at applying intermarket data (as well as fundamental data) to market forecasting.

For instance, for a neural network designed to forecast New York Light Crude Oil, the analysis includes ten years of past price, volume and open interest data on crude oil futures.

The analysis also includes the following intermarket inputs: crude oil cash, the Bridge/CRB Futures Price Index, the S&P 100, Comex gold, Comex silver, the Japanese yen, N.Y. heating oil #2, Treasury bonds and the U.S. Dollar Index. Additionally, fundamental data inputs can be incorporated. Once the raw input data has been selected, it is preprocessed using various algebraic and statistical methods of transformation, in order to facilitate learning.

## The Hidden Layer

The hidden layer is used by a neural network for internal processing to store its "intelligence" during the learning process. This layer is composed of neurons where the network recodes the input data into a form that captures hidden patterns and relationships. The network generalizes from previously learned facts to new inputs, which allows it to make its forecasts. The number of neurons in the hidden layer and the number of hidden layers are determined through experimentation.

## The Output Layer

The output layer is where a network's forecasts are made. Two types of real number outputs in financial analysis include forecasts of prices such as the next day's high and low, and forecasts of technical indicators such as a predicted 5-day moving average value for two days in the future. Decisions must be made about not only what output to forecast, but also how far into the future to make the forecast.

## Learning Algorithms

There are many different learning algorithms that can be used to train a neural network. Each algorithm has different performance characteristics. All of the algorithms attempt to minimize the overall error in the network's forecasts.

One popular learning algorithm is the gradient-descent algorithm. However, gradient-descent trains slowly and often finds sub-optimal solutions. This limitation is similar to pitfalls encountered with back-testing and optimization of rule-based trading strategies in which sub-optimal sets of parameter values are found that are isolated and unstable.

## How a Neural Network Learns

Training a neural network involves a repetitive mathematical process in which the neural network learns underlying hidden patterns, discerns leads and lags and identifies nonlinear relationships within the data from repeated exposures to the input data. Learned information is stored by the network in the form of a weight matrix, with changes in the weights occurring as the network "learns." Similar to the learning process people engage in, a neural network learns patterns by being exposed to repeated examples of them. Then the neural network generalizes through the learning process to related but previously unseen patterns.

One popular network paradigm that has been used for financial market analysis and forecasting is known as a "feed-forward" network that trains through "back-propagation of error" which is depicted in Figure 6-2.

Once trained, a neural network acts as a market forecasting tool, allowing traders to achieve the trend identification and forecasting goals of technical analysis.

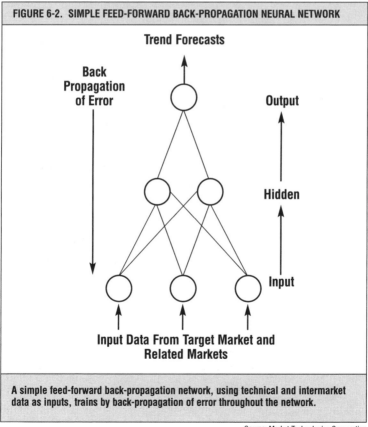

FIGURE 6-2. SIMPLE FEED-FORWARD BACK-PROPAGATION NEURAL NETWORK

Trend Forecasts

Back Propagation of Error

Output

Hidden

Input

Input Data From Target Market and Related Markets

A simple feed-forward back-propagation network, using technical and intermarket data as inputs, trains by back-propagation of error throughout the network.

Source: Market Technologies Corporation

## Overtraining Is Not Desirable

Overtraining a neural network must be avoided. Overtraining occurs when a neural network memorizes the subtleties and idiosyncrasies particular to specific training data, without developing the capacity to generalize to new data. Overtraining is analogous to curve-fitting or over-optimization when performing back-testing and optimization on rule-based trading strategies. An overtrained network will perform poorly on out-of-sample test data and subsequently when making its forecasts during realtime trading.

## How a Neural Network Is Tested for Accuracy

Testing is performed by creating an independent test file made up of data that had not been seen by a neural network during the training process. In the testing mode the neural network is given these new inputs and utilizes the representation that it had previously learned to generate its forecasts. This allows the network to be evaluated under simulated trading conditions. This is analogous to "walk-forward" or "out-of-sample" testing of rule-based trading strategies.

Performance results from various neural networks on test data can be compared prior to making a determination about which specific neural network to select for use in the final application. Depending on the comparative test performance results, changes often need to be made in the selection of input data, preprocessing, network architecture, etc., and retraining conducted before the final application network is selected.

## There's More to Neural Networks

There are similarities and differences between designing and training a neural network and developing and testing rule-based trading strategies. If you want to learn more about the technical details and underlying mathematics behind neural networks, I refer you to my personal website *www.FutureForecasts.com* which includes reprints of many of the research articles and book chapters I have previously written about the application of neural networks to technical analysis and market forecasting.

# Chapter 7

## THE NEXT HORIZON
### Where Do We Go From Here and What Does This Mean for Traders?

As the world's financial markets become increasingly integrated, intermarket analysis will play a crucial role in market analysis in the first decades of the 21st century, just as backtesting and optimization of single-market trading strategies became integral to computerized technical analysis in the late 20th century.

The narrow single-market approach that analyzes each individual market based upon its own internal past price data must be supplanted by a multi-dimensional approach. A decade ago I referred to the synthesis of technical, intermarket and fundamental approaches as "synergistic market analysis." No financial market is an island. They are now all integrally linked to one another.

Fortunately, neural networks are not only well-suited to analyzing markets from both a single-market as well as an intermarket perspective, but can also incorporate fundamental data inputs. These might include supply and demand statistics, and economic data such as the Gross National Product, the Producer Price Index, the Consumer Price Index and Unemployment statistics. Even comparative economic statistics from different countries can be included.

In effect, as the financial markets continue to evolve, technical analysis, intermarket analysis and fundamental analysis will blend together, creating the three-legged stool known as financial market analysis.

By utilizing the computational modeling capabilities of neural networks in a structured framework that integrates seemingly disparate

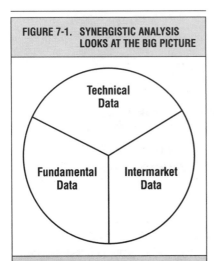

**FIGURE 7-1. SYNERGISTIC ANALYSIS LOOKS AT THE BIG PICTURE**

Technical Data

Fundamental Data

Intermarket Data

The next phase in the evolution of technical market analysis will be "synergistic market analysis," combining technical, intermarket and fundamental data. This completes the three-legged stool of financial market analysis, covering the entire global economic and financial landscape.

Source: Market Technologies Corporation

technical, intermarket and fundamental data as depicted in Figure 7-1, quantitative trend forecasting will continue to be at the cutting-edge of financial market analysis in the 21st century.

History is replete with accounts of newly emerging technologies, which have subsequently had a major impact on economic development and the financial markets—making early adopters wealthy in the process. The railroad, the airplane, the telephone, xerography, and the Internet represent such technologies, with substantial commercial applications, which have become part of the economic landscape.

Technological progress cannot be forestalled by those who are skeptical, inflexible or simply too afraid to adopt something new or different. Such close-mindedness and shortsightedness is an anachronism in today's rapidly changing technology-driven world.

Within the financial industry, the same can be said for the application of advanced quantitative technologies such as neural networks and intermarket analysis to global financial market analysis and trading. In the past, new analytical innovations involving the application of quantitative technologies have met resistance within the financial industry. In the future, though, as emerging technologies demonstrate their effectiveness they will become more quickly incorporated into the practice of financial market analysis.

Neural networks are real; they work, and they are here to stay. Still, they are just one of the mathematical tools applicable to the implementation of synergistic trading strategies. Other tools, including expert systems, genetic algorithms, fractal geometry, chaos theory and fuzzy logic to name a few, are also being applied to market analysis with varying degrees of success. There is certainly much more to come!

## There Will Never Be a Financial Crystal Ball

My research and development efforts will continue to be focused on increasing VantagePoint's forecasting accuracy. Some of the factors that are under study involve the inclusion of additional global markets to be considered as intermarket inputs and the optimization of the size of the moving average lengths and look-forward periods that are used to make the trend forecasts.

In addition, I intend to develop additional VantagePoint programs to monitor financial markets outside of the United States such as Short Sterling on the London International Financial Futures Exchange and the Euroyen on the Singapore Exchange Ltd. I am also interested in applying intermarket analysis to individual large-cap equities comprising the Nasdaq-100 Index and assessing the impact of incorporating fundamental data inputs into VantagePoint.

Obviously, there will never be a financial crystal ball that traders can gaze into to see what the markets will do in the future with 100% accuracy. In my opinion it will not be possible for market analysts to predict trend direction with more than 80-85% accuracy, due to randomness and unpredictable events that are inherent in the global financial markets, as well as the difficulty of developing effective forecasting tools.

With VantagePoint's current accuracy level over 70% on all twenty-five markets monitored, over 75% on fourteen of them, and over 80% on two of them (the 5-year Treasury notes and gas oil), VantagePoint is already within striking distance of what is *realistically attainable* in terms of forecasting accuracy.

Even then, there are a myriad of additional factors such as mass psychology, judgment, trading experience, risk propensity, fear, greed, money management and amount of capital that affect one's trading performance.

I am determined to push the forecasting envelope as far as it will go. It's my passion. This is what has made the financial markets and technical analysis so emotionally exciting, intellectually challenging and financially compelling to me.

Right now, a robust, yet easy-to-use, intermarket analysis tool such as VantagePoint is a smart way for serious traders to fill the gap in their technical analysis arsenals so they can start benefiting immediately from intermarket analysis without having to reinvent the wheel or study to become rocket scientists.

As more traders embrace intermarket analysis and incorporate it into their trading, they will be able to make winning market trades based on the hidden relationships and complex patterns between related markets, reflecting the *market synergy* behind today's global markets.

I hope that this book has helped make you more aware of the implications that the globalization of the financial markets has on your own trading, and am confident that by broadening your perspective to include intermarket analysis, whether you are a stock, options or futures trader, you will be able to improve your trading performance and self-confidence to make more decisive and profitable trading decisions.

If you have any questions concerning any of the information covered in this book, please feel free to contact Market Technologies Corporation by e-mail at *IMA@ProfitTaker.com* or through its website at *www.ProfitTaker.com* where you can learn more about intermarket analysis, neural networks and VantagePoint.

At the website, you can also examine actual up-to-date Vantage-Point Daily Reports for various financial markets, which will show you in more detail how VantagePoint can benefit you. Additionally, you can register on the website to receive free e-mail alerts from Market Technologies Corporation. You can also contact Market Technologies Corporation by telephone at 800-732-5407 or 813-973-0496 or by fax at 813-973-2700.

# Trading
# Resource
# Guide

▲▲▲▲▲▲

## TOOLS FOR SUCCESS
## IN TRADING

# Trading Resource Guide

## The Visual Investor: How to Spot Market Trends
*by John J. Murphy*

Track the ups and downs of stock prices by visually comparing charts—instead of relying on complex formulas and technical concepts. Introduces readers to Intermarket Analysis—a proven analytical approach based on evaluating the impact different markets have on each other. Includes a software disk and instructions for using charts and graphs.

$50.00   Item #T211X-2379

## Intermarket Technical Analysis: Trading Strategies for the Global Stock, Bond, Commodity, and Currency Markets
*by John J. Murphy*

Take technical analysis to the next plateau with help from one of America's top technical analysts. You'll learn how global markets affect one another, and how to use technical analysis combined with fundamental information to spot—and exploit—market opportunities.

$75.00    Item #T211X-2397

## Technical Analysis Simplified
*by Clif Droke*

Here's a concise, easy-reading manual for learning and implementing this invaluable investment tool. The author distills the most essential elements of technical analysis into a brief, easy-to-read volume. Droke's compact guide is a great starting place—and the perfect complement to any technical analysis software program.

$29.95   Item #T211X-11087

# Trader's Guide to Technical Analysis

*by C. Colburn Hardy*

Achieving high-impact results can be made easier by implementing the most effective technical analysis tools throughout your trading day. In this easy-to-read classic, you will learn when to buy and sell stocks with the help of technical analysis—written for the average investor.

You will also learn to recognize trends and pinpoint entry points, and how to improve trading results by combining technical and fundamental tools and techniques.

$37.50   Item #T211X-11563

# Technical Analysis of Stock Trends, 8th Edition

*by Edwards, Magee and Bassetti*

The universally acclaimed investor's classic has now been updated with the latest data and references. With more than 800,000 copies in previous editions, this is the definitive reference on analyzing trends in stock performance. It incorporates the most recent stock information and updated charts for expert guidance.

$99.95   Item #T211X-17379

# Technical Analysis of the Financial Markets

*by John J. Murphy*

From how to read charts to understanding indicators and the crucial role of technical analysis in investing, you won't find a more thorough or up-to-date source. Revised and expanded for today's changing financial world, it applies to both equities and futures markets.

$70.00   Item #T211X-10239

# The ARMS Index

*by Richard Arms, Jr.*

Get an in-depth look at how volume—not time—governs market price changes. Describes the Arms' short term trading index (TRIN), a measure of the relative strength of the volume in relation to advancing stocks against that of declines. A true market gem.

$39.95   Item #T211X-3130

# Encyclopedia of Chart Patterns

*by Thomas N. Bulkowski*

In addition to utilizing various indicators that help identify trends, there is a multitude of chart patterns in this new book that will tell the analyst whether the stock or commodity is in a bullish or bearish mode. Also included in this book are patterns tell the analyst what the stock is going to do based on where its price has been.

$79.95   Item #T211X-10781

# Trade Your Way to Financial Freedom

*by Van K. Tharp*

Deeper than the usual "tell all" book.  Tharp shows novice and experienced traders alike how to carefully craft a trading plan to achieve both long and short-term goals and, ultimately, financial freedom.

$29.95   Item #T211X-10245

# Dow 100,000: Fact or Fiction

*by Charles W. Kadlec and Ralph J. Acampora*

This book will help you anticipate the upcoming bright financial future and to design investment strategies that are coherent with your financial goals.

$25.00   Item #T211X-11612

# New Era of Wealth: How Investors Can Profit From the 5 Economic Trends Facing the Future

*by Brian Wesbury*

Filled with fascinating case histories, solid research, and innovative investing strategies—this book will cut short the pessimists and doomsayers, change the way you view your place in the new economy, and send you into the new millennium armed with a wealth-building program designed to minimize your long term risk and maximize your return.

$24.95    Item #T211X-10612.

# The Roaring 2000's

*by Harry Dent*

It is essential to understand the nature of the forces changing our economy in order to take advantage of the emerging investment opportunities. This book will serve as a profit and risk guide for the new millennium.

$25.00    Item #T211X-10694.

# Important Internet Sites

**Traders' Library Bookstore** . . . . . . . . . . www.traderslibrary.com
The #1 source for trading and investment books, videos and related products.

**Louis Mendelsohn** . . . . . . . . . . . . . . www.FutureForecasts.com
Includes information about Louis Mendelsohn, his personal library of articles, speeches, and book contributions, all available online.

**American Stock Exchange** . . . . . . . . . . . . . . www.amex.com
Provides current market activity on equities, indexes, options and Amex index shares, online tutorials and brochures on investing.

**Chicago Board Options Exchange** . . . . . . . . . . www.cboe.com
Provides market data on indexes and stocks, quotes, charts, company reports, market commentary, and information on options trading.

**Chicago Board of Trade** . . . . . . . . . . . . . . . . www.cbot.com
Provides news, market information, background on the exchange and various educational programs and seminars offered by the CBOT®.

**Chicago Mercantile Exchange** . . . . . . . . . . . . . www.cme.com
Provides a wealth of information including price data, contract specifications, a news center, and background on the Merc.

**MurphyMorris** . . . . . . . . . . . . . . . . . www.murphymorris.com
The site of John J. Murphy, which offers extensive information on technical analysis and intermarket analysis.

**TheStreet.com** . . . . . . . . . . . . . . . . . . . . . www.TheStreet.com
Provides both individual and professional investors with timely, to-the-point financial news and analysis needed succeed in today's markets. Updated before, during and after the bell by the best independent financial newsroom on the Web. Find programs from some of the best financial minds in the business - including Alan Farley, Gary Smith, Jim Cramer and over 25 popular columnists on RealMoney.com.

**NASDAQ Stock Exchange** . . . . . . . . . . . . . . . www.nasdaq.com
Provides news headlines, earnings calls and calendar, portfolio
tracking, information on international and sector indexes, stock
screening, and information on the Nasdaq-100 Index Tracking
Stock QQQ.

**New York Mercantile Exchange** . . . . . . . . . . . www.nymex.com
Provides information on energy seminars and conferences,
quotes, contract specifications.

**New York Stock Exchange** . . . . . . . . . . . . . . . . www.nyse.com
Provides market quotes, a personal stock tracker and information
on listed companies, IPOs and equities trading.

# Learn More About
# VantagePoint Software
## Trend Forecasting and Market Timing Technology

▲ ▲ ▲ ▲ ▲ ▲

## Discover how you can stack the odds in your favor with VantagePoint Software — and its amazing forecasting capabilities . . .

It is no longer sufficient for traders to focus internally on single-markets in isolation of what related markets are doing. A new aspect of technical analysis, known as intermarket analysis, has become a critical ingredient to successful trading. To be competitive, traders must now have a broad intermarket perspective and the necessary analysis tools to implement it. VantagePoint Intermarket Analysis Software will give you a road-map — showing you what it expects the market to do — thereby giving you the self-confidence to take trades that should be taken — and keep you *out* of marginal trades that should be avoided.

## VANTAGEPOINT:

- Monitors major financial markets
- Five neural networks make independent forecasts
- Reports offer detailed analysis on past and future forecasts
- Intermarket charts show you what's ahead

## VantagePoint anticipates trends — it does not follow them!

VantagePoint was designed by traders who understand that to be successful in today's markets, you need to have a "heads up" on what is *most likely to happen in each market tomorrow*, not just what it has done today or in the past! With VantagePoint's forecasting capabilities, each day you'll know — with near-ly 80% proven accuracy:

- What trend direction is anticipated over the next two to four days
- Tomorrow's expected high/low
- Whether the market is expected to make a *top* or *bottom*

## *Plus . . .* VantagePoint is quick and easy to use

- VantagePoint is ready to use when you receive it.
- You do NOT need to know anything about intermarket analysis or neural networks.
- You don't even need to know anything about programming. Unlike other complicated software programs, VantagePoint is easy to use and lets you *focus on trading* instead of getting distracted by the complexities of the software itself.
- The Daily Update function within VantagePoint automatically processes VantagePoint's five neural networks, which then generate their forecasts for the next day's trading. All you do is compare the Daily Reports (or charts) for several target markets to see which markets offer the best trades to take the next day. The process takes **only a few minutes** from start to finish.

## What more do you need to be successful?

Discover the power of this amazing software program — and start stacking the odds in your favor today. Call now for full details.

## Call 800-732-5407 Extension 100
### www.ProfitTaker.com/93110

MARKET
TECHNOLOGIES CORP.

# About the Author and Market Technologies Corporation

▲ ▲ ▲ ▲ ▲ ▲

Louis B. Mendelsohn is president and chief executive officer of Market Technologies Corporation. Mr. Mendelsohn began trading equities in the early 1970s, followed by stock options. Then, in the late 1970s he started trading commodities, as both a day and position trader. In 1979 he formed Market Technologies Corporation to develop technical analysis trading software for the commodity futures markets.

In 1983, Mendelsohn pioneered the first commercial strategy backtesting and optimization trading software for microcomputers. By the mid-1980s these capabilities became the standard in microcomputer trading software for both equities and futures, fueling the growth of today's multi-million dollar technical analysis software industry.

Recognizing the emerging trend toward globalization of the world's financial markets, in 1986 Mr. Mendelsohn again broke new ground in technical analysis when he created the first commercial intermarket analysis software in the financial industry for microcomputers.

Building on his extensive research in the 1980s involving intermarket analysis, in 1991 Mendelsohn released VantagePoint Intermarket Analysis Software, which makes short-term market forecasts based upon the pattern recognition capabilities of neural networks. Since then, Mendelsohn's research has continued to focus on intermarket analysis and market forecasting. In addition to his research, software development and corporate management responsibilities, he actively trades in the financial markets.

Mr. Mendelsohn has written extensively since 1983 in many prominent financial publications including *Barron's*®, *Futures*, and *Technical Analysis of Stocks & Commodities*™. He has been widely quoted in the financial media including *The Wall Street Journal* and *Investor's Business Daily*, has collaborated on more than half a dozen books on technical analysis, and has been interviewed live on national radio and television, including CNBC, CNNfn and Bloomberg Television.

Mendelsohn has also spoken at numerous financial conferences and symposia, including the Futures Industry Association annual meeting, Futures Symposium International, the Harvard Business School Alumni Club, Futures Truth and the Annual Meeting of the Association for Investment Management and Research.

Due to his achievements in the application of computers and information technologies to technical analysis over the past quarter-century, his biography is included in Marquis *Who's Who in the World*®, *Who's Who in America*®, and *Who's Who in Finance and Industry*®. He has been a full member of the Market Technicians Association since 1988, and is a colleague of the International Federation of Technical Analysts.

Born in 1948 in Providence, Rhode Island, Mendelsohn received a B.S. degree in Administration and Management Science from Carnegie Mellon University in 1969, an M.S.W. degree from the State University of New York at Buffalo in 1973, and an M.B.A. degree with Honors from Boston University in 1977.

Since its founding by Mr. Mendelsohn, Market Technologies Corporation has been at the forefront of development of state-of-the-art technical analysis tools and information technologies for the financial markets. Located in the Tampa Bay region of Florida since 1979, the firm has individual and institutional clients in over thirty countries throughout the world.

Market Technologies Corporation was recently ranked the 29th fastest growing private corporation in Florida, out of the top one-hundred companies in the *Florida 100* competition based on three-year revenue growth, sponsored by the University of Florida, Deloitte & Touche LLP, PricewaterhouseCoopers LLP, and Raymond James & Associates, Inc.

Market Technologies Corporation was also ranked the 17th fastest growing technology company in Tampa Bay, based on five-year revenue growth, out of the top fifty public and private technology firms in the *Tampa Bay Technology Fast 50* competition, sponsored by Deloitte & Touche LLP.

**COMPANY INFORMATION:**
Market Technologies Corporation
E-mail address: IMA@ProfitTaker.com
Website address: www.ProfitTaker.com
Phone: 800-732-5407 or 813-973-0496
Fax: 813-973-2700
25941 Apple Blossom Lane
Wesley Chapel, Florida 33544

# Free 2 Week Trial Offer for U.S. Residents From Investor's Business Daily:

I NVESTOR'S BUSINESS DAILY will provide you with the facts, figures, and objective news analysis you need to succeed.

*Investor's Business Daily* is formatted for a quick and concise read to help you make informed and profitable decisions.

To take advantage of this free 2 week trial offer, e-mail us at customerservice@traderslibrary.com or visit our website at www.traderslibrary.com where you find other free offers as well.

You can also reach us by calling 1-800-272-2855 or fax us at 410-964-0027.

This book, along with other books, are available at discounts that make it realistic to provide them as gifts to your customers, clients, and staff. For more information on these long lasting, cost effective premiums, please call John Boyer at 800-424-4550 or e-mail him at john@traderslibrary.com